CORETTA SCOTT
KING

CORETTA SCOTT KING

Lisa Renee Rhodes

CHELSEA HOUSE PUBLISHERS
Philadelphia

Chelsea House Publishers

Editor-in-Chief	Stephen Reginald
Managing Editor	James D. Gallagher
Production Manager	Pamela Loos
Art Director	Sara Davis
Picture Editor	Judy Hasday
Senior Production Editor	Lisa Chippendale

Staff for CORETTA SCOTT KING

Senior Editors	John Ziff
	Therese DeAngelis
Associate Editor	Kristine Brennan
Associate Art Director	Takeshi Takahashi
Designer	Brian Wible
Picture Researcher	Patricia Burns
Cover Illustrator	Earl Parker

First Printing

1 3 5 7 9 8 6 4 2

Library of Congress Cataloging-in-Publication Data

Rhodes, Lisa Renee.
Coretta Scott King / by Lisa Renee Rhodes.
144 pp.   cm. — (Black Americans of achievement)
Includes bibliographical references (p. 138) and index.
Summary: Biography of Martin Luther King's widow, from her childhood in
rural Alabama to her crusade to keep her husband's message of peace and
equality alive after his murder in 1968.
ISBN 0-7910-4690-7. — ISBN 0-7910-4691-5 (pbk.)
1. King, Coretta Scott, 1927-   —Juvenile literature. 2. Afro-American
women—Biography—Juvenile literature. 3. Afro-Americans—Biography—
Juvenile literature. 4. Civil rights workers—United States—Biography—
Juvenile literature. 5. Civil rights movements—United States—History—
20th century—Juvenile literature. 6. King, Martin Luther, Jr., 1929-1968—
Juvenile literature.
[1. King, Coretta Scott, 1927-   . 2. King, Martin Luther, Jr., 1929-1968. 3.
Civil rights workers. 4. Afro-Americans—Biography. 5. Women—Biography.
6. Civil rights movements.] I. Title. II. Series
E185.97.K47R56 1997
323'.092—dc21
[B]
                                                                97-36364
                                                                CIP
                                                                AC

Frontis: *In the decades since her husband's assassination, Coretta Scott King has proven to be an tireless activist for causes ranging from world peace to racial equality.*

CONTENTS

BLACK AMERICANS OF ACHIEVEMENT

❧

HENRY AARON
baseball great

KAREEM ABDUL-JABBAR
basketball great

MUHAMMAD ALI
heavyweight champion

RICHARD ALLEN
*religious leader and
social activist*

MAYA ANGELOU
author

LOUIS ARMSTRONG
musician

ARTHUR ASHE
tennis great

JOSEPHINE BAKER
entertainer

JAMES BALDWIN
author

BENJAMIN BANNEKER
scientist and mathematician

AMIRI BARAKA
poet and playwright

COUNT BASIE
bandleader and composer

ROMARE BEARDEN
artist

JAMES BECKWOURTH
frontiersman

MARY MCLEOD BETHUNE
educator

GEORGE WASHINGTON
CARVER
botanist

CHARLES CHESNUTT
author

BILL COSBY
entertainer

PAUL CUFFE
merchant and abolitionist

MILES DAVIS
musician

FATHER DIVINE
religious leader

FREDERICK DOUGLASS
abolitionist editor

CHARLES DREW
physician

W. E. B. DU BOIS
scholar and activist

PAUL LAURENCE DUNBAR
poet

DUKE ELLINGTON
bandleader and composer

RALPH ELLISON
author

JULIUS ERVING
basketball great

LOUIS FARRAKHAN
political activist

ELLA FITZGERALD
singer

MARCUS GARVEY
black nationalist leader

JOSH GIBSON
baseball great

WHOOPI GOLDBERG
entertainer

ALEX HALEY
author

PRINCE HALL
social reformer

JIMI HENDRIX
musician

MATTHEW HENSON
explorer

BILLIE HOLIDAY
singer

LENA HORNE
entertainer

WHITNEY HOUSTON
singer and actress

LANGSTON HUGHES
poet

ZORA NEALE HURSTON
author

JESSE JACKSON
civil-rights leader and politician

MICHAEL JACKSON
entertainer

JACK JOHNSON
heavyweight champion

MAGIC JOHNSON
basketball great

SCOTT JOPLIN
composer

BARBARA JORDAN
politician

MICHAEL JORDAN
basketball great

CORETTA SCOTT KING
civil-rights leader

MARTIN LUTHER KING, JR.
civil-rights leader

LEWIS LATIMER
scientist

SPIKE LEE
filmmaker

CARL LEWIS
champion athlete

JOE LOUIS
heavyweight champion

RONALD MCNAIR
astronaut

MALCOLM X
militant black leader

BOB MARLEY
musician

THURGOOD MARSHALL
Supreme Court justice

TONI MORRISON
author

ELIJAH MUHAMMAD
religious leader

EDDIE MURPHY
entertainer

JESSE OWENS
champion athlete

SATCHEL PAIGE
baseball great

CHARLIE PARKER
musician

ROSA PARKS
civil-rights leader

COLIN POWELL
military leader

PAUL ROBESON
singer and actor

JACKIE ROBINSON
baseball great

DIANA ROSS
entertainer

WILL SMITH
actor

CLARENCE THOMAS
Supreme Court justice

SOJOURNER TRUTH
antislavery activist

HARRIET TUBMAN
antislavery activist

NAT TURNER
slave revolt leader

DENMARK VESEY
slave revolt leader

ALICE WALKER
author

MADAM C. J. WALKER
entrepreneur

BOOKER T. WASHINGTON
educator

DENZEL WASHINGTON
actor

OPRAH WINFREY
entertainer

TIGER WOODS
golf star

RICHARD WRIGHT
author

ON
ACHIEVEMENT

———— ❦ ————

Coretta Scott King

Before you begin this book, I hope you will ask yourself what the word *excellence* means to you. I think it's a question we should all ask, and keep asking as we grow older and change. Because the truest answer to it should never change. When you think of excellence, perhaps you think of success at work; or of becoming wealthy; or meeting the right person, getting married, and having a good family life.

Those goals are worth striving for, but there is a better way to look at excellence. As Martin Luther King Jr. said in one of his last sermons, "I want you to be first in love. I want you to be first in moral excellence. I want you to be first in generosity. If you want to be important, wonderful. If you want to be great, wonderful. But recognize that he who is greatest among you shall be your servant."

My husband knew that the true meaning of achievement is service. When I met him, in 1952, he was already ordained as a Baptist minister and was working toward a doctoral degree at Boston University. I was studying at the New England Conservatory and dreamed of accomplishments in music. We married a year later, and after I graduated the following year we moved to Montgomery, Alabama. We didn't know it then, but our notions of achievement were about to undergo a dramatic change.

You may have read or heard about what happened next. What began with the boycott of a local bus line grew into a national crusade, and by the time he was assassinated in 1968 my husband had fashioned a black movement powerful enough to shatter forever the practice of racial segregation. What you may not have read about is where he learned to resist injustice without compromising his religious beliefs.

He adopted a strategy of nonviolence from a man of a different race, who lived in a different country and even practiced a different religion. The man was Mahatma Gandhi, the great leader of India, who devoted his life to serving humanity in the spirit of love and nonviolence. It was in these principles that Martin discovered his method for social reform. More than anything else, those two principles were the key to his achievements.

These books are about African Americans who served society through the excellence of their achievements. They form part of the rich history of black men and women in America—a history of stunning accomplishments in every field of human endeavor, from literature and art to science, industry, education, diplomacy, athletics, jurisprudence, even polar exploration.

Not all of the people in this history had the same ideals, but I think you will find that all of them had something in common. Like Martin Luther King Jr., they all decided to become "drum majors" and serve humanity. In that principle—whether it was expressed in books, inventions, or song— they found a goal and a guide outside themselves that showed them a way to serve others instead of living only for themselves.

Reading the stories of these courageous men and women not only helps us discover the principles that we will use to guide our own lives; it also teaches us about our black heritage and about America itself. It is crucial for us to know the heroes and heroines of our history and to realize that the price we paid in our struggle for equality in America was dear. But we must also understand that we have gotten as far as we have partly because America's democratic system and ideals made it possible.

We are still struggling with racism and prejudice. But the great men and women in this series are a tribute to the spirit of the country in which they have flourished. And that makes their stories special and worth knowing.

1
WIDOW

Happily married to a prominent Baptist minister and the mother of four beautiful children, Coretta Scott King had many blessings to count on Thursday, April 4, 1968. Experience had taught her to guard against becoming complacent about anything life had given her, though. Specifically, life with her husband, the Reverend Dr. Martin Luther King Jr., made Coretta aware—at times painfully so—that hers would never be an ordinary family.

That spring day had begun uneventfully enough, however. Coretta was busy taking care of her children in her Atlanta, Georgia, home. She looked forward to Easter, which was only a few days away. Her husband was on an important trip, but she and the children expected to spend the holiday with him upon his return.

Coretta had finished all of her pre-holiday shopping with the exception of selecting some dresses for her 12-year-old daughter, Yolanda. Although she initially had had some misgivings about buying the children new clothes for Easter because she feared that the sacred meaning of the holiday would be lost, she had relented with Martin's blessing. With everything else the children faced—including long separations from their father—she decided to spare them from feeling left out at Easter services, where everyone would be displaying their new finery.

Although her husband's sudden death thrust multiple responsibilities onto her shoulders, Coretta Scott King's first priority was consoling her children. Here she cradles her youngest child, five-year-old Bernice, during funeral services for Martin Luther King Jr.

Coretta and Yolanda went shopping in down-town Atlanta that afternoon. They had just come home when the telephone rang. Jesse Jackson, a young minister from Chicago, was on the line.

"Coretta, Doc just got shot," Jackson said. "I would advise you to take the next thing smoking."

Coretta's heart stood still. "Doc" was her hus-band, Dr. King.

As Jackson explained that Martin had been shot in the shoulder, Coretta tried not to imagine the worst. She hung up the phone and called her best friend, Dora McDonald. She then made arrangements to catch the next plane to Memphis, Tennessee, where her husband lay wounded. Dr. King had been sched-uled to lead a march there to protest the treatment of the city's garbage collectors, who were demanding better wages and work conditions.

Andrew Young, another black minister, called Coretta from Memphis a few minutes later. Reverends Young, Jackson, and Ralph Abernathy, all of whom worked with Dr. King, had planned to take part in the protest march. Young's news about Martin's condition was more accurate than Jackson's had been: Dr. King, he reported, was in serious condition with a gunshot wound to the neck.

News of the shooting was important not only to his family. Millions of Americans flocked to their televisions and radios to learn the details of the trag-ic event. For 12 years, Dr. King had led a nonviolent protest movement to win equal rights for black Americans and end a 400-year-old legacy of racial prejudice and injustice in the United States. African Americans were treated like second-class citizens because state and federal laws failed to guarantee them the rights enjoyed by whites, particularly in the southern United States. A threat to King's life was a threat to the entire civil rights movement.

Coretta turned on the television in her living room. Reports of the shooting had already reached

news stations across the country. Yolanda and her siblings, Martin III, 10, Dexter, 7, and little Bernice, 5, came into the living room. Coretta didn't want them to learn of their father's fate from a television report, but Yolanda, the oldest, already realized that something serious had happened to her father and ran crying from the room. She returned shortly, and Coretta told all of her children the news. "I'm getting ready to go to Memphis, because your daddy has been shot," she said. Yolanda helped her mother pack her bags.

Ivan Allen, the mayor of Atlanta, called and offered to escort Coretta to the airport. Family, friends, and neighbors rushed to the Kings' home as soon as they heard about the shooting. Coretta tried to remain calm: she knew she couldn't fall apart in front of the children.

But it was not Coretta Scott King's nature to fall

When Coretta brought Martin's body back to Hanley's Funeral Home in Atlanta, she wanted her children (left to right: Yolanda, Bernice, Martin III, and Dexter) to see it so that they would understand that their father had been permanently taken from them.

apart. She had stood bravely by the side of Dr. Martin Luther King Jr. for all of the 14 years they had been married. Their marriage was the foundation of a public crusade against racism.

Coretta and Martin grew up at a time when state and federal laws kept southern blacks from living in the same neighborhoods as whites. The laws also prohibited blacks and whites from attending the same public schools and eating in the same restaurants. And blacks had no voice in changing the laws: through various means they were routinely denied the right to vote.

Dr. King's leadership helped to end racial segregation. He and a group of black ministers and community leaders formed a civil rights organization called the Southern Christian Leadership Conference (SCLC) to work for social justice. Dr. King and the SCLC organized marches, boycotts, and other protests to convince southern whites—and the entire nation—that racist laws, behavior, and attitudes were immoral. Dr. King and his followers risked being arrested, beaten, mocked, and even lynched to prove their point. But they never raised a hand to their tormentors because Dr. King believed that the struggle for equal rights had to be won without violence.

Coretta also believed in nonviolence and in the right of blacks and all Americans to live in dignity and peace. Her deep religious faith had helped her face many ordeals during the struggle for civil rights—times when Dr. King was jailed and even one instance when he was stabbed. Coretta knew that justice could be won, and she understood that sacrifices were necessary to achieve it. But now she wondered if her husband's life had to be one of those sacrifices.

Coretta kissed her children good-bye and left them in the care of friends as she departed for the airport. Dr. King's sister Christine King Farris and her husband, Isaac; Mayor and Mrs. Allen; and local minister Rev. Fred Bennette and his wife left with Coretta. Dora McDonald promised to meet them all at the airport.

Coretta hurried along the airport's corridor to find the gate for her flight. But before she boarded the plane, her name was called over the public address system. "I had a strange, cold feeling," Coretta recalled in her autobiography, *My Life with Martin Luther King, Jr.*

Coretta asked Mayor Allen to send someone to the public information station for her. "Of course I already knew," she wrote, "But it had not yet been said. . . . I was trying to make myself believe that Martin was dead."

Coretta and her companions got the news moments later. Martin Luther King Jr. was indeed dead, at only 39 years old. With her own 41st birthday just 23 days away, Coretta was now a widow.

Through her tears and those of the people with her, Coretta decided that her first order of business was getting home to her children. The ride back from the airport was silent; no one knew what to say.

Once home, Coretta put the children to bed, but stayed awake for hours herself. When Yolanda asked her, "Mommy, should I hate the man who killed my daddy?" Coretta replied, "No, darling, your daddy wouldn't want you to do that." Then she had to steel herself against breaking down when seven-year-old Dexter asked her when his daddy would return.

Telephone conversations were no easier. Dr. King's parents were devastated when they heard the news. Martin Luther King Sr., a prominent Baptist minister and respected black leader in Atlanta, could not believe his son was dead. "I always felt I would go first," the elder King lamented to Coretta.

The King family's telephone rang continually for hours. President Lyndon Johnson called to express his condolences, as did Senator Robert Kennedy, brother of the late President John F. Kennedy. Several years before, President Kennedy and Robert Kennedy, then U.S. attorney general, had helped to protect Dr. King and his followers during their protests. A phone call from Robert Kennedy once helped to gain King's release from prison after he was arrested for refusing to give his seat to a white person at a lunch counter in 1960.

Coretta knew she had to fly to Memphis to bring her husband's body back home. Senator Kennedy offered to provide a plane. He also ordered additional telephones to be installed in the King home so Coretta and her family could respond to the flood of phone calls that would surely come in as the news of Dr. King's death spread across the nation.

The next day, Coretta and some friends flew to Memphis. Dr. King's body was taken to Hanley's Funeral Home when they arrived back in Atlanta. Coretta asked the funeral director to open the casket so her children could see their father's body. She hoped this would help five-year-old Bernice (Bunny), in particular, to understand that her father was not coming home.

Dr. Martin Luther King Jr. was shot while he stood on the balcony of the Lorraine Motel in Memphis. A white man named James Earl Ray allegedly fired a rifle from a room in a boarding house across from the motel. The bullet left a gaping hole in King's right jaw.

The Reverend Ralph Abernathy, Dr. King's closest friend and colleague, had been with Martin moments before his death. On that tragic evening, Abernathy and Samuel B. Kyles, a minister from Memphis, were standing with King on the balcony outside of his bedroom at the Lorraine Motel. They were getting ready to attend a local civil rights meeting with several other SCLC members. Abernathy left the balcony and went into the bedroom to put on some aftershave. Kyles headed downstairs to the motel parking lot.

Martin Luther King Jr. (second from right) and his associates, (left to right) Hosea Williams, Jesse Jackson, and Ralph Abernathy on the balcony of the Lorraine Motel on April 3, 1968. Tragedy would strike in that very spot the next day.

As King stood alone on the balcony, the sound of a gunshot shattered the stillness. Alarmed, Abernathy rushed to the door of the balcony and saw King lying on his back. The balcony was stained with blood. Abernathy ran to his friend's side. King moved his lips, but he could not speak. One hour later, he was dead.

The thousands of black Americans and others who had followed Dr. King and the civil rights movement were shocked at the news of his untimely death. They wondered how anyone could shoot Dr. King—a man whose life was dedicated to peace and justice. The crime left them angry and disillusioned. Many also feared that the struggle for civil rights was over. Who would lead the Memphis march in King's place? What would become of the SCLC? There were many unanswered questions and troubled hearts in the wake of the assassination. Some of this pain, Coretta noted, translated into "an ironic tribute" to her nonviolent husband—rioting in 63 U.S. cities.

Family and close friends did all they could during this sorrowful time. Entertainer Harry Belafonte, a friend of the King family and a supporter of the civil rights movement, flew to Atlanta to offer

Coretta his help.

She began to make arrangements for her husband's funeral. Years before, he had won the Nobel Peace Prize for his dedication to nonviolence and his belief in the equality of all people. His nonviolent protest movement had touched the lives of countless people in America and around the world. Coretta wanted Martin's funeral to pay homage to his spiritual strength and moral courage.

Harry Belafonte suggested that Coretta make some sort of public statement to comfort Dr. King's followers and to answer questions from the press. He also requested her help in leading the protest march for the garbage collectors in Memphis, which was still scheduled for Monday, April 8. Belafonte urged Coretta to participate, telling her it would mean a lot to the movement and to the nation if she would come. Coretta knew there was a chance of violence at the march. Dr. King's death was strong evidence that deep racial hatred still existed in America. In fact, enemies of the civil rights movement had already warned the SCLC that they would disrupt the protest march. SCLC members also worried that they would be stopped from demonstrating by a federal injunction.

But Coretta was not afraid. She agreed to go because she believed it was her duty to talk to the people and to march with them. She also knew her husband would have wanted it no other way. Before Coretta left for Memphis, Dr. King's body was prepared for burial. The funeral would take place on Tuesday, April 9—the day after the Memphis march. King's casket was placed in the Sister's Chapel at Spelman College, an all-black women's college in Atlanta, for a few days before the funeral. Coretta permitted this so that people throughout the city could pay their respects to the slain leader. Coretta made her speech on the Saturday before her husband's funeral. The site was Ebenezer Baptist

Church, where Martin Luther King Sr. pastored for more than 30 years. It was the King family's church throughout Martin's childhood, and Dr. King eventually joined his father as its copastor. These strong family ties made Ebenezer the perfect place for Coretta to give her speech.

"My husband faced the possibility of death without bitterness or hatred," Coretta said. "He never hated. He never despaired of well-doing. And he encouraged us to do likewise, and so he prepared us constantly for the tragedy. . . . Our concern now is that his work does not die."

Coretta thanked the SCLC, the Ebenezer Church, family, friends, and Dr. King's followers across the country and the world for their support. She told the people of her plans for the funeral and invited all well-wishers to attend. The leadership of the SCLC would pass on to the Reverends Ralph Abernathy and Andrew Young.

On Monday, Coretta and her children flew to Memphis to lead the march for the garbage collectors. More than 25,000 people marched with the King family, Rev. Abernathy, and other members of the SCLC to city hall. Despite the threats, there were no disruptions or incidents of violence. The marchers and onlookers remained silent throughout the protest in tribute to Dr. King.

Coretta and her children stood on the platform at city hall. As usual, Coretta was composed and dignified. "My spirit has been uplifted because so many thousands of persons and followers of my husband, like you, have done so many wonderful things," she said. "Your presence here today indicates your devotion." Coretta urged the people not to give up. She asked them to continue believing in Dr. King's movement and in the principles that had guided his life. She also asked them to follow his example—to sacrifice the comforts of life for causes that would benefit all humankind. Violence had never solved any prob-

UNSTOPPABLE MAN

At the urging of Harry Bela-fonte (left), Coretta and her three oldest children led a protest march through Memphis on April 8, 1968, in Martin's honor. The message on the movie-theater marquee ironically footnoted King's short life.

lems and it would not bring Dr. King back, she reminded the crowd.

Her words soothed the hearts and minds of the marchers, who were also inspired to see Coretta standing tall despite her loss. People who opposed the goals of the civil rights movement—social justice for black Americans and equality for all oppressed peoples—were given a subtle warning. Coretta Scott King was not afraid to go to any city, state, or country to spread her husband's message of love and peace. She would not be moved by threats.

Political, religious, and civic leaders from all over the country and people from all racial, ethnic, and economic backgrounds flocked to Atlanta's Ebenezer Baptist Church on the day of Dr. King's funeral. Only a fraction of those who wanted to attend could actually fit into the 750-seat church. Coretta wore a black dress, a sheer black veil, and black gloves. Her quiet strength was evident in the way she gently guided her children through the solemn service.

Dr. King's favorite gospel hymns filled the air.

Friends gave speeches and paid tribute to his life and work. A tape of one of his last sermons was played for all to hear. His voice soothed Coretta's broken heart.

When the funeral service was over, Coretta and her family led thousands of mourners in a march from the church to Morehouse College for a final memorial service. Dr. King had graduated from Morehouse, an all-black men's college, in 1948. His casket was carried to the college on a farm wagon that was pulled by two mules. Coretta chose this method of transportation to represent her husband's dedication to the plight of the poor.

Dr. Benjamin Mays, Martin's lifelong mentor, gave the eulogy. He expressed great love and admiration for the slain civil rights leader and thanked God for giving America and the world such a faithful servant of peace and justice.

At last, Dr. Martin Luther King Jr. was laid to rest. Rev. Abernathy performed a brief burial ceremony. Coretta watched in silence as her husband's casket was placed inside a crypt deep in Atlanta's soil.

The newly widowed Coretta comforted her children and family. She also accepted condolences from Dr. King's followers and friends all over the world. Although too busy to be consumed by her grief in the months after Martin's death, Coretta still battled pain and loneliness. A few weeks after the funeral, she flew to New York to take Martin's place at a peace rally. Using notes her husband had left behind, she wrote a speech for the event. As she spoke, Dr. King's message became her own.

Coretta grieved, but her mind was set on a goal: she wanted no one to forget the life and work of Dr. Martin Luther King Jr. She turned her sorrow and pain into action, working tirelessly to preserve her husband's place in history as a courageous and effective activist for civil rights.

Coretta Scott King once walked the road to freedom with her husband. Now she would walk it alone.

2
THE SCOTTS

❦

Coretta Scott was born on April 27, 1927, in Heiberger, a small, rural, segregated town in Alabama. Blacks in Heiberger and in Marion—the nearest city at 12 miles away—outnumbered whites two to one. Heiberger was a farming community, and few families worked harder at farming than the Scotts.

Coretta's grandfather, Jeff Scott, owned 300 acres of land that he shared with his children and grandchildren. Coretta was named after her deceased grandmother Cora. Although Coretta never met Cora, it was often said that she had inherited her grandmother's determination. Cora had helped Jeff become a prosperous farmer and an important religious and civic leader in Heiberger's large black community.

Jeffrey and Cora's son, Obadiah, married Bernice McMurry in 1920. Obadiah and Bernice built a two-room house on the Scotts' farm, where they raised their three children. Coretta, her older sister Edythe, and her younger brother Obie shared a bedroom with their parents. The children slept in one bed; Obadiah and Bernice, in another. A fireplace heated the

Black workers hoe cotton in Alabama during the 1920s. Although slavery had ended more than 50 years before Coretta's birth in the rural town of Heiberger, she picked cotton on white-owned farms to earn money as a child.

room. The Scotts cooked meals on a wood-burning stove and they got water from a well. They had an outhouse instead of a bathroom.

Coretta grew up in meager surroundings, but her family was rich in other ways. The Scotts were hard-working and devout Christians. Obadiah Scott set a strong example for his children. A proud man, he refused to let racism break his spirit. He woke up early every morning to take logs and timber to the town's sawmill. The sawmill was owned and operated by whites, but Obadiah was the only black man in town who owned the truck he drove. When he and Bernice married, he was earning three dollars a day hauling timber, but by the time the sawmill operator had deducted what he wanted from Obadiah's pay, and Obadiah had made the loan payment for his truck, there was little money to spare. To make ends meet, he worked as a barber at his home on weekends. Bernice helped him by cutting and shaving a few customers whenever the line grew long outside of their makeshift barbershop.

Every Sunday, the Scotts attended Mount Tabor A.M.E. (African Methodist Episcopal) Zion Church. Grandfather Scott, a steward of the church and chairman of the board of trustees, also oversaw the Sunday school service for children. All of the Scott clan and other black families from miles around would flock to Mount Tabor to hear the Christian gospel. People came to lay down their burdens and find comfort in the church's message of forgiveness and hope. Some were so moved by the Sunday service that they shouted for joy and cried.

Coretta's maternal grandfather, Martin McMurry, was a singer. He led the church choir and the congregation in gospel songs.

Martin McMurray's granddaughter shared his love for music. At home, Coretta turned on her parents' big Victrola and listened to songs of all styles, from gospel to jazz.

When she wasn't listening to music, Coretta could be found playing outside with her siblings and cousins. Like other girls her age, she wore her hair in braids, but she was a tomboy underneath her feminine exterior. She enjoyed playing games, but didn't like being teased—and could put up an extraordinary fight if her brother Obie dared to torment her. Coretta had a fiery temper. She feared no one and stood up for herself often—character traits destined to serve her well as an adult.

Coretta started working on the farm when she was six or seven years old. She helped her mother plant, hoe, and harvest corn, peas, and potatoes. Her chores also included feeding chickens and hogs and milking cows. The Scotts lived off of the crops and livestock they raised on the farm. Nothing was wasted by the family, for that would have been a grievous sin.

Coretta's mother had worked on a farm when she was a child, too. Bernice's parents also owned land in Heiberger, and she completed only four grades in school because her parents needed her to plant and harvest crops. Bernice's father, Grandfather McMurry, who was part Native American, claimed to have attended school for "about two days in his life." But he had learned to read a little bit by studying the Bible. Mrs. McMurry, a talented seamstress, sewed clothes for her children and grandchildren.

When Coretta was about 10, she started working in the cotton fields. Slavery had ended more than 50 years before her birth, but the economy of the southern United States still depended on cotton. In the early 1930s, southern blacks were still hired by whites to harvest it. The Scotts and other families worked in the fields during the fall to make extra money. Cotton pickers could earn up to five dollars in one season. One year, Coretta managed to make an impressive seven dollars in the cotton fields. She, Edythe, and Obie used the extra money to pay for textbooks and school supplies.

The church was one place where southern blacks could attain positions of respect and authority during the early 20th century. Both of Coretta's grandfathers were prominent members of Mount Tabor A.M.E. Zion Church, which was probably very similar to the building pictured here.

Picking cotton to help earn a living was a symbolic reminder of the dark days of slavery, when blacks toiled in the fields for no wages. Blacks in Alabama and throughout the South continued to be degraded and victimized, despite the fact that their forebears were freed—first in principle when President Abraham Lincoln signed the Emancipation Proclamation in 1863, then in reality when the Civil War ended two years later. African Americans were free, but not equal; they still had few of the civil rights that white Americans enjoyed. If a black person was accused of a crime, for example, he or she could not get a fair trial in a southern courtroom. Although cases involving black defendants went to trial in accordance with the law, white judges and juries were often biased, handing down more convictions and stiffer penalties to blacks than to whites.

It was against this oppressive backdrop that Coretta's parents instilled in her the values of honesty, hard work, and thrift. The fact that their daugh-

ter was growing up at a time when stereotypes por-
trayed blacks as untrustworthy, lazy, and given to
theft compounded the difficulty of their task.

Self-sufficient black Americans like Coretta's
father were considered a threat—particularly to poor
whites. Whites who had little education and who
struggled to make ends meet often blamed blacks for
their plight. They resented any black person who
lived well, regardless of how much sacrifice and hard
work it had taken to do so. Furthermore, rich and
poor southern whites alike would commonly address
a black man as "boy" and a black woman as "girl."
Black adults seldom were called by their given
names—even by white children. Southern Blacks
were treated so badly that few would dare even to
look a white person in the eye. To do so was to risk
death.

Black men were particularly vulnerable. It was
not safe for a black man to walk or drive alone late at
night. In the morning he might be found dead, the
victim of hanging, burning, or some other grisly form
of mutilation.

This exceedingly heinous type of murder is called
lynching. Whites who lynched blacks were seldom
arrested. One of Coretta's great-uncles was lynched,
shot to pieces by white men. In her autobiography,
Coretta marveled that her successful father "did not
end up in a swamp because of his obvious self-
respect."

Grandfather Scott, who had instilled such
strength in his son, could point to remarkable accomplishments for a black man who was born just 10
years after the end of slavery and who lived in the
hostile environment of the Deep South. He sold
insurance for a living and owned an automobile. He
also traveled around the country attending important
religious and civic meetings.

Grandfather Scott's and Grandfather McMurry's
leadership roles in the church exemplified the type

of authority that black men could hold in the South. Many black men served as ministers and passed their duties on to their sons. The church was a safe haven for African Americans, one of the few places where they were shielded from insults and the threat of death.

Their churches were among the few institutions in the community that blacks could own. Since most rural blacks lived in poverty, it was extremely difficult for them to become business owners. But a small number of blacks were able to finish elementary and high school. Some even went on to all-black colleges or religious or liberal schools that were usually reserved for white students. These African Americans were able to become doctors, lawyers, and teachers who provided their services to the black community.

Coretta learned about the injustice of racism in school. She and Edythe attended a two-room wooden elementary school that housed more than 100 black children in grades one through six. Two black women taught all of the students, using a wall covered with black paint as a blackboard. The school had no library, and all of the children had to buy their own textbooks. Therefore, the money Coretta and Edythe made from cotton picking was very important: they would have been unable to complete even the simplest homework assignments without the books it enabled them to purchase. The school had an outhouse rather than an indoor bathroom.

Every morning, Coretta and Edythe walked three miles to school. The white children in Heiberger rode a school bus, however. Their school was a sturdy brick building and their textbooks were free.

But the teachers at the black school inspired the Scott girls with their genuine concern for the students and their strenuous efforts to educate them despite a lack of resources. Coretta later credited one of her elementary teachers, Mrs. Mattie Bennett, with recognizing and encouraging her and Edythe's eagerness to learn.

Their mother also encouraged the girls to become voracious learners. "You get an education and try to be somebody," Bernice once told Coretta. "Then you won't have to be kicked around by anybody, and you won't have to depend on anyone for your livelihood—not even on a man."

Coretta was an excellent student. Mrs. Bennett also encouraged her to develop her talent for singing by selecting Coretta to be the school's song leader. Coretta sang solos on special occasions and also read poetry out loud to her classmates. When she grew older, she sang in church and performed solos in front of the congregation.

In 1938, Coretta graduated from elementary school at the top of her sixth-grade class. Edythe had graduated two years earlier and had enrolled in Lincoln High School, one of the most progressive schools in Marion. Edythe was one of the few blacks in Heiberger to finish high school. Years before, their father had gone to Lincoln, but he completed only a year because he had to work.

Coretta followed Edythe to Lincoln High, a semiprivate school that had been started by white missionaries after the Civil War to help educate blacks. The school's founders held a philosophy that urged equality and social justice for all Americans, regardless of race. Lincoln's faculty included blacks and whites, but all of the students were black. Although the school's tuition may not sound like much today—$4.50 per child—the Scotts had to tighten their purse strings to send their daughters to Lincoln. But they knew Edythe and Coretta would benefit by learning in an environment that fostered academic and personal excellence.

Obadiah's hard work was paying off in many ways. Not only could he afford his children's education, but he also rented a new and larger home for his family.

The year before Coretta graduated from elementary school, the Scotts moved into a six-room house, complete with new furnishings. Sending Edythe and Coretta to Lincoln was just one more blessing.

Coretta started high school when she was 12 years old. Her admission to Lincoln marked the beginning of a long journey toward personal independence and intellectual development.

Lincoln was 10 miles away from home, so Edythe and Coretta lived with a black family in Marion. It was the first time the girls had lived away from their parents. In Marion they also interacted with whites on a regular basis for the first time.

Coretta flourished in school. She studied music under the tutelage of Miss Olive Williams, a black woman who had graduated from Howard University in Washington, D.C., and who specialized in classical music and voice. Although Coretta sang in elementary school and the church choir, she could not read music, and her voice was not formally trained. But with Miss Williams' guidance, Coretta learned to read music, play the piano, and sing classical works such as the Messiah oratorio by George Frideric Handel. She also learned to play the trumpet while at Lincoln.

Edythe also studied music. She joined the Lincoln School Little Chorus and traveled around the country singing in special concerts.

Coretta admired and looked up to her older sister. In many ways, Edythe was the trailblazer in the Scott family. As the oldest child, she was expected to succeed and set an example, just as her father had. Obie was a few years younger than his sisters, but he followed in their footsteps and attended Lincoln.

The white teachers at Lincoln treated Edythe, Coretta, and the other students with respect; but life outside of school was a different story. White youths in Marion harassed the black students as they walked to and from school. Coretta always felt uneasy when the white students came around. She never knew what would happen. The whites often tried to start fights by calling the blacks "niggers" and pushing them off the sidewalk. But for the most part, the black students refused to be bullied. They held their heads high and walked in a group so no one could be singled out.

Coretta worked part-time after school cleaning house for a white woman, an experience she found troubling. The woman insisted that Coretta call her "Ma'am" and that she enter the house through the back door. "I did not last long in her employment," Coretta recalled.

The threat of lynching was a constant in the lives of Coretta's male relatives. Sometimes, lynchings were committed by Klansmen like the one shown here; but disorganized groups of whites might also shoot, hang, burn, or mutilate a black man unfortunate enough to be caught alone at night.

In 1941, the county school board began to pay some of the costs of transporting black students to school. The new funding made it possible for Coretta to live at home during her junior and senior years at Lincoln. Obadiah, who now owned three trucks, donated one of them to the community to use as a school bus. Bernice became the bus driver.

Coretta was happy to be home. She directed the church choir and played piano during Sunday services. During the week, she led rehearsals for the youth choir.

The Scotts' prosperity made some whites in Heiberger furious. Obadiah's financial independence, his community service, and his children's accomplishments were shining examples of black achievement. Obadiah Scott was getting "too big for his britches" in the opinion of some disgruntled whites.

In the fall of 1942, while Edythe and Coretta were at school, the local undertaker called to tell them the bad news that the Scotts' new home had burned to the ground. The family moved in with Grandfather McMurry, who was now a widower.

The next day, Obadiah went to work as if nothing had happened. No one knew how the fire had started, and the police never investigated.

After the fire, Coretta's father seemed more determined than ever. He continued to haul timber and, by the spring, had saved enough money to buy his own sawmill. Obadiah hired a white logger to work for him. Not long after, the white man asked to buy the sawmill, but Obadiah refused his offer.

When Obadiah went to work a few days later, the sawmill was burned to the ground. Unbowed, Obadiah drove timber to another man's sawmill the next morning.

In her autobiography, Coretta recalled the time when a white man had accused her father of owing $100 in unpaid debts for a car accident that had occurred around 1937. Obadiah knew that he had already met his financial obligation in the matter, but he agreed to make the extra payment anyway.

When he was finally out of debt, Obadiah came home from work with $40 in cash and treated his family to a shopping spree in Marion. It was not buying new merchandise, but rather Obadiah's joy at once again being "a man who could run his own affairs" that was cause for celebration. Coretta remembered this episode as proof of the Scott family's resilience and strength. These traits were her family's legacy to Coretta.

3

MISS CORETTA

ntioch College, a small liberal arts institution surrounded by the lush grass and trees of Yellow Springs, Ohio, was founded in 1852. Horace Mann, the college's first president, fought against slavery and believed that educated men and women of all races could make America a better place to live.

Edythe enrolled at Antioch on a one-year scholarship after she graduated as Lincoln High School's valedictorian in 1943. At that time Antioch was one of the few American colleges to offer educational opportunities to women and blacks. As one of the first black students to attend the college full-time, Edythe was herself a pioneer.

Edythe had first visited Antioch as a member of the Lincoln School Little Chorus, which performed at the college during a concert tour. The faculty and administrators were impressed with the quality of Lincoln's students and a few years later, Antioch contacted Lincoln and several other predominantly black high schools in the South to offer a few scholarships to qualified students. The Scotts encouraged Edythe to apply. She was intelligent, creative, and outspoken—a strong candidate for any college.

When Edythe won a scholarship to Antioch, the Scotts were thrilled. Their firstborn child was going to college! For southern blacks, higher education was the route to personal and professional pros-

Coretta as a junior at Antioch College. She later credited her undergraduate education with giving her "a new self-assurance that encouraged me in competition with people of all racial, ethnic, and cultural backgrounds."

35

Coretta Scott as a student at Antioch College in 1945.

perity. Institutions in the northern United States were viewed as places where people of color could fulfill their academic promise free from the limitations and sorrows of racial discrimination. Obadiah and Bernice hoped that a college education and a chance to establish roots in the North would ensure Edythe a better life.

Coretta was next in line for college, although she wasn't sure where she would enroll. But she was sure that, like her sister, she wanted to leave the South.

When Edythe was settled at school, she wrote occasional letters to Coretta, who read them with wide-eyed wonder. She learned about Antioch's open atmosphere and academic honor system. The students worked with teachers to design their own course of study, and they learned to become independent thinkers and risk-takers. The faculty trusted students to make their own decisions and to be responsible young adults. Antioch's beautiful campus was also a plus. "You'd love it here, Coretta," Edythe wrote.

When Coretta thought seriously about college, it didn't take her long to choose Antioch. At Lincoln, she had refined her musical skills. But she looked forward to the chance to learn and do still more—especially at a college where she could be with her older sister, whom she admired very much. By the time Coretta applied for admission in the spring of 1945, Edythe was a sophomore. If Coretta was accepted at Antioch, her sister could help her find her way as a college student.

Coretta was awarded a $450 partial scholarship to attend Antioch. Her family had to pay an additional $200 for tuition and expenses.

Coretta enrolled at the college in the fall of 1945. The move from Alabama to Ohio was quite an adjustment, and Coretta's first year of classes was very hard. Her study habits were not to blame: in fact, she later described herself as a "grind"—someone who allocated little time to anything but studying. Despite her glowing high school record, Coretta wrote in My Life with Martin Luther King, Jr. that, "like most southern students, I had such an inadequate education that even Lincoln had not prepared me properly."

To remedy the problem, Coretta signed up for a remedial reading class in her second semester at Antioch. The extra instruction helped Coretta keep up with the grueling college curriculum. She later reflected on her eventual success, writing, "In a sense, I made more progress than some of the students who came with more advantages, because I had so far to go to catch up."

In addition to coursework, Antioch students were expected to participate in the college's community work program in order to graduate. Students alternated one semester of classes with a semester of work experience. At the end each work semester, every student had to write an evaluation of his or her job experience to receive a grade.

During the summer of her freshman year, Coretta worked as a junior music counselor at the Karamu Camp. The camp was operated by the Karamu House of Cleveland, an organization dedicated to bringing people of different races and ages together through music and the arts. In her sophomore year, Coretta worked for five months at the Friendly Inn Settlement House, a similar organization located in one of Cleveland's poorest neighborhoods.

Coretta broadened her study of music, adding the violin to her list of instruments. She also continued her study of music theory, voice, piano, and choral arts. She was becoming a proficient singer and musician. Walter Anderson, the only black member of Antioch's faculty, was a professor of music. He encouraged Coretta's thirst for knowledge and dedication to her craft. Jessie Treichler, a student counselor, was also fond of Coretta. Anderson and Treichler became her mentors, supporting Coretta's musical and academic efforts. Years later, Coretta would recall one of the highlights of her studies—the chance to perform in a musical program with Paul Robeson, a celebrated African-American singer and actor. Robeson was so moved by Coretta's singing that he encouraged her to continue her studies and to pursue a professional career.

The academic schedule at Antioch kept students busy. In her early years at the college, Coretta was a bit shy, although all of the students were polite and congenial. Coretta and Edythe were two of only six black students on campus, however. Coretta felt subtle signs of prejudice among white students. "People were nice to me and tried to be friendly," she recalled years later. "But I could sense that in the back of their minds there was a feeling of race superiority bred in them through generations and by all the myths about black people [that] they had acquired."

These subtle hints of racial inequality convinced Coretta that despite Antioch's liberal aspirations, there was an invisible division between the few blacks and the numerous whites on campus. Years later, Coretta would recall that white students considered her and her black peers to be "exceptions" to their race—rare examples of black Americans who were not as lowly as the rest. "Of course, you're different, Corrie," some white students would say.

But Coretta had been unaware of any racial unease at Antioch when she applied for admission. Edythe never mentioned any hardships in her letters. She was careful not to complain, sharing only positive news with her younger sister.

In time, Coretta learned that Edythe had a difficult time being a black pioneer on a mostly white campus. Social conversations with white students always revolved around issues of race, despite the fact that Edythe, being only one person, could never speak for her entire race. In her autobiography, Coretta described Edythe as having become "awfully tired of discussing the Negro's problems at breakfast, lunch, and dinner." The social pressure Edythe felt to be "The Black Student" made it hard for her to be herself.

Dating was not easy for Edythe, either. Although young men at Antioch found her "tall and attractive" sister an engaging lunch companion, Coretta reported that "Edythe dated only white fellows on two occasions" during her entire time at Antioch.

By the time Coretta was a sophomore, Edythe had left Antioch to enroll at Ohio State University for her senior year. The university had a larger black student population, and Edythe felt more comfortable there. Although saddened by her sister's departure, Coretta also confessed, "It was not until my sister had gone to take her senior year at Ohio State that I came into my own."

Coretta declared a double major in music and

Walter Anderson was one of Coretta's mentors at Antioch. Anderson was a music professor who recognized and encouraged her considerable talent.

Coretta later wrote that her sister Edythe (shown here) had gotten "awfully tired of discussing the Negro's problems at breakfast, lunch, and dinner" with her white peers while at Antioch. Edythe also found dating on campus difficult.

elementary education in her junior year. She became Antioch's first black education major.

The college's student-teaching program required education majors to teach for one year at Antioch's private elementary school and then for another year in the public school system. For Coretta's first year of practice, she taught music at the Antioch school. For her second year of practice, however, Coretta was barred from teaching in the Yellow Springs public schools because of her race.

Although the Yellow Springs public school system was integrated, all of the teachers were white. When the supervisor of Antioch's student-teaching program advised Coretta not to make a fuss over the issue, she was outraged. How could something like this happen in a place that was supposedly racially tolerant?

Coretta remembered what her father had told her whenever he was confronted by racism: "If you look a white man in the eye, he can't hurt you."

She decided to fight back, making an appointment with the college president to plead her case. But after listening disinterestedly to her complaint, the president replied, "Well, Corrie, what do you want us to do about it?"

Coretta suggested that the college protest the school system's decision and make an appeal on her behalf to the Yellow Springs school board. The college president refused, though, and Coretta was given two choices. She could teach in a segregated black school in another town, or she could teach for another year at Antioch elementary school.

Coretta refused to teach in the segregated school, proclaiming, "I came here from Alabama to be free of segregation." Despite her hurt and disappointment, she consented to teach at Antioch's school for another year. Like her father Obadiah had before her, Coretta used this painful experience to fuel her determination to excel. The episode became a turning point rather than an utter defeat. She later wrote that it also strengthened her resolve to help others:

> I said to myself, "Now, I'm going to be a Negro for the rest of my life, and I have to face these problems. So I'm not going to let this one get me down. I'll have to accept a compromise now, but I don't have to accept it as being right. I'm going . . . to do something about this situation. I don't want those who come after me to have to experience the same fate as I did."

Coretta's first step was to join the college's Race Relations and Civil Liberties Committees and its chapter of the National Association for the Advancement of Colored People (NAACP). Coretta became active in campus functions that advocated

Coretta as a student at Boston's New England Conservatory of Music. Life as a self-supporting woman in a large northern city was an exhilarating adventure for a girl from humble beginnings in rural Alabama.

the equality of all people.

In addition to activism, music helped to soothe her spirit. Coretta made her debut as a singer at the Second Baptist Church in Springfield, Ohio, in 1948. She later returned to the church to perform as a guest soloist. In 1950, she performed recitals in Pennsylvania and sang at her alma mater, Lincoln

High School.

Antioch College showed Coretta the best of what higher education could offer, as well as its serious shortcomings. She was able to take advantage of opportunities for advancement that were not commonly available to women of any race in the 1940s. Coretta overcame academic obstacles and blossomed into a professional singer. She also deepened her Christian commitment to helping others through community service.

But Coretta also faced a deceptive form of racial prejudice and cowardice that spoiled the lives of blacks who lived in the North. Unlike the blatant racism of the South, northern discrimination was often subtly disguised by social customs and public policies—even among people who professed liberal attitudes toward blacks. For example, Coretta had staunchly refused to date the one black man in her college class—mainly because other Antioch students automatically saw him as her ideal escort because of his race.

Coretta's college experiences helped her to grow stronger, wiser, and more mature. By the time she graduated from Antioch in 1951 with a bachelor of arts degree in music and elementary education, Coretta was no longer the quiet, naive young girl who had arrived from Heiberger, Alabama, on the coattails of her older sister.

"Antioch gave me an increased understanding of my own personal worth," Coretta wrote in *My Life with Martin Luther King, Jr.* years later. "I enjoyed a new self-assurance that encouraged me in competition with all people of all racial, ethnic, and cultural backgrounds, on their terms or on mine."

Coretta's newfound confidence helped her decide to pursue a career in music. She enjoyed teaching but felt her true calling was to be a concert singer. Professor Anderson encouraged her to apply to the New England Conservatory of Music in

Boston to continue her vocal studies. Mrs. Treichler helped Coretta apply for financial aid from the Jessie Smith Noyes Foundation.

Coretta was accepted at the conservatory, but the Noyes Foundation had placed her name on a waiting list of students who qualified for a grant. She spent the summer of 1951 with her family and friends in Alabama. By this time, Obadiah owned a general merchandise store, which he had purchased in 1946. Coretta had worked part-time for her father during the summer while she was in college; after graduation, she again helped in the store.

By the fall, Coretta was ready to head north with or without a scholarship. She boarded a train to Boston without asking her parents to help her pay for her schooling. Coretta wanted to remain independent. She took with her only the money she had saved over the summer. Meanwhile, Mrs. Treichler made arrangements for Coretta to stay with Mrs. Bartol, a wealthy Bostonian who gave generous donations to Antioch. Mrs. Bartol lived in Beacon Hill, one of Boston's most affluent neighborhoods.

When Coretta arrived in Boston, she received word from her family that she had won a $650 grant from the Jessie Smith Noyes Foundation to cover full-time tuition at the New England Conservatory of Music. "My prayers had been answered!" Coretta later wrote of the news. Mrs. Bartol agreed to provide housing and breakfast for seven dollars a week. Coretta was grateful for a place to stay, but she knew she would have to find a job to pay for her housing.

By the time she settled in Mrs. Bartol's home, Coretta had only $15 left from her savings. She had enough money to pay for her transportation to school, but she had to cut back on her total expenses. Accordingly, one of her first meals in Boston was a supper of graham crackers, peanut butter, and fruit.

Mrs. Bartol and Coretta soon made a business

deal. Coretta agreed to help clean the fifth-floor bedrooms, halls, and stairways in exchange for a room and breakfast. The extra work helped to relieve Coretta's financial worries to some extent, but she still had to afford her other meals and expenses. She talked Mrs. Bartol into letting her help with the laundry for extra money.

The New England Conservatory of Music was one of the top music conservatories in the United States. Studying there would give Coretta the chance to perfect her abilities as a concert singer in a professional setting. She hoped someday to perform with orchestras and other ensembles. But Coretta was one of no more than 20 black students at the conservatory, and was the only black living on her block in Beacon Hill. The social isolation was difficult, but Coretta was able to handle it gracefully—thanks to her college years. She was determined not to let racial segregation stand in her way.

After several weeks in Boston, Coretta found a part-time job at a mail-order company. She couldn't have been happier with how things were falling into place. She was pursuing her professional aspirations, paying her own way, and making her own decisions. In her autobiography, Coretta's recollection of her first days in Boston crackle with the enthusiasm of a young woman striking out on her own. "All these years I had waited," she wrote, "and now I was here in Boston in this environment where I was absorbing music. Everything about it seemed so right."

What Miss Coretta Scott did not realize was that soon, she would meet someone who would force her to rethink the future she had so carefully planned.

4

DR. AND MRS. MARTIN LUTHER KING JR.

꧁꧂

Martin Luther King Jr. also seemed to have his life very much in order. When he was 15 years old, Martin had begun his studies at Morehouse College, an all-black men's school in Atlanta, where he became the protégé of Dr. Benjamin Mays, a Baptist minister and the college president. Mays used the church's pulpit to denounce racial segregation and to call on black men to reclaim their dignity. At 18, Martin himself was ordained a Baptist minister and became his father's assistant pastor at Ebenezer Baptist Church, one of the most socially progressive black churches in Georgia. Before enrolling in Boston University's School of Theology to pursue a Ph.D. in the fall of 1951, Martin had been valedictorian of his graduating class at Crozer Seminary in Pennsylvania, earning a bachelor's degree in divinity.

At 22, Martin Luther King Jr. was a well-educated and accomplished young man who also had a reputation for charm and sociability. But there weren't many young blacks in Boston, so people tended to date close friends or associates. Many young adults met at church or at private parties.

Mary Powell, the wife of a nephew of Dr. Benjamin Mays, thought Coretta and Martin would make a perfect pair. Mary, who graduated from Spelman College, knew Martin from Morehouse. She had met and befriended Coretta at the conservatory.

In My Life with Dr. Martin Luther King, Jr., Coretta recounted having been unimpressed by her first glimpse of Martin. He, on the other hand, was immediately smitten with her.

47

So when Martin asked Mary if she knew any eligible young ladies after he settled in Boston, Mary mentioned Coretta. She in turn gave Coretta a glowing description of Martin's endeavors as a "very brilliant" young minister.

Coretta was somewhat put off by Martin's profession: she instantly recalled the narrow-mindedness of some ministers she had known. "Genuine piety is inspiring," she wrote in her autobiography, "but many ministers I had met went around wearing a look of sanctity that they seemed to put on like their black suits." But Coretta hadn't heard about Martin's charming demeanor. While it was true that he was a very studious minister, he was no sanctimonious bookworm. Martin—or M. L., as friends and family called him—was known for his sense of humor and his ease in meeting new people. But Boston did not readily afford him the companionship of southern ladies, and he wanted to meet someone with style and charm.

When Martin finally called Coretta at home, his wit, engaging personality, and lively conversation began to change her mind about ministers—a little bit. Martin talked about his theology studies, while Coretta talked about her music lessons. Martin was easy to talk to and didn't seem boring. He also managed to make Coretta laugh a few times, which was a good sign. He asked Coretta for a lunch date and she consented to go. Martin agreed to pick her up the next day in front of the conservatory, playfully telling her that he would speed up the 10-minute drive and complete it in 7 just for her.

Their lunch date fell on a wet, cold January day. Coretta wore a wool knit light blue suit and a black winter coat. "I still remember everything I was wearing that day," she later wrote. She curled her bangs, wore her hair on her shoulders, and applied a touch of lipstick. It was never her style to dress in a flashy manner.

Martin arrived at 12:00 sharp in a bright green Chevrolet. Coretta thought he looked "short" and "unimpressive" seated behind the wheel. Although it wasn't love at first sight, Coretta was open and polite.

Over lunch, Coretta's impressions of Martin slowly began to change. She found him thoughtful, well spoken, and extremely intelligent. The more Coretta listened, the taller Martin seemed to become in her eyes.

Coretta was a bit nervous, but Martin's charm helped put her at ease. She talked not only about her own studies, but also gave her opinion on important social issues. Martin was not shy about his feelings on the drive back to the conservatory. He thought Coretta Scott was quite a catch and he told her so. "You have everything I ever wanted in a wife," Martin said, citing Coretta's character, intelligence, personality, and beauty. "I want to see you again. When can I?"

Although startled by Martin's comments, Coretta played it cool. "I don't know. I'll have to check my schedule," she replied. "You may call me later."

When Coretta got home, she wasn't sure what to think. Marriage? She and Martin had just met! Coretta wasn't involved with anyone at the time and she was in no rush to start a romance. In her personal affairs, Coretta had always been selective and cautious.

Her refusal while in college to date the only black man in her class just because others expected her to do so was a prime example of Coretta's unwillingness to be led into a situation without careful consideration. She could not stand the idea of establishing relationships with blacks only, thereby letting other people's racial assumptions determine her friends and companions. As a result of her strong-mindedness, Coretta hadn't dated at Antioch until her junior year. A fellow music student—a bright young Jewish man—had asked her out on a

Martin Luther King Jr. (seated left) credited his parents, Alberta Williams King (standing left) and Martin Luther King Sr. (standing center), with instilling in him "a sense of somebodiness" as he grew up in Atlanta during the 1930s. Maternal grandmother Jennie Williams stands on the right. Seated with Martin are his sister Christine and brother Alfred Daniel.

date. They ended up dating for a year until he graduated.

Coretta was unsure about starting a relationship with Martin, especially a serious one that could lead to marriage. Her music studies and future career came before any personal commitments. "I had resolved not to become emotionally entangled again until I was absolutely certain," she later remembered.

Yet Coretta knew that M. L. was very special. Although she feared eventually compromising her career by becoming involved with him, she also already knew that she would see him again. "I rationalized it by telling myself that he was such a fine young man, that I would wait and see what happened," she admitted in her autobiography.

But Martin Luther King Jr. was a man who had never lived his life using a wait-and-see approach. Born on January 15, 1929, in Atlanta, Martin seemed to possess both an adventurous spirit and a startlingly mature sense of direction from an early age. He loved to play pranks on his older sister Christine and younger brother Alfred Daniel, or A. D. He was an excellent student who skipped grades 9 and 12 in high school. Despite his small stature, he was also a fierce competitor in sports, eventually playing quarterback for Morehouse's football team.

Unlike Coretta, Martin didn't know what it was like to grow up poor. His father, Martin Luther King Sr., or Daddy King, was a Baptist minister and self-made businessman who had risen from poverty to provide his family with a solidly middle-class standard of living. Martin Sr. married Alberta Williams in November of 1926. They moved into a 12-room house that Alberta inherited when her father, also a minister, died suddenly five years later. Reverend Williams had been pastor of Ebenezer Baptist Church. When he died, Martin Sr. took over his father-in-law's pastoral duties. Reverend King became an outspoken advocate for the rights of southern blacks, even leading a group of blacks in a voter registration drive in 1935. By the time his children were born, Rev. King was highly respected in the black community.

Alberta King was the church's music director. When her children grew older, she hired a music teacher to give them piano lessons at home. Martin never picked crops or worked on a farm as a child, although he did have chores to do around the house. He also held one job as a newspaper boy during his childhood.

But racism was a childhood experience that Martin and Coretta had in common. As in other southern cities, racial segregation was a way of life in Atlanta. When Martin entered school, he was sent to a segregated elementary school, while several white playmates in the neighborhood went to school elsewhere. The parents of the white children abruptly decided after this to forbid their children from associating with a "colored boy." Once, Martin's father refused to buy shoes at a white-owned store because a clerk told him to sit in the back in order to be served. Daddy King stormed out, dragging young M. L. by the hand and vowing never to accept such treatment quietly.

Years later, when Martin recalled his childhood, he said he grew up with "a sense of somebodiness." Like Obadiah and Bernice Scott, the Kings instilled an unshakable sense of self-confidence in their children. Martin never saw his parents weaken under the weight of racism.

By the time Martin was a teenager, he was known as an impressive public speaker. At 14, he had won a prize in an oratory contest for a speech called "The Negro and the Constitution." By 15, Martin was on his way to college after he passed a special test for admission to Morehouse. Three years later, he became assistant pastor at Ebenezer Baptist Church, where he shared the pulpit with his father.

In My Life with Martin Luther King, Jr., Coretta recalled that Martin was unsure of the purpose of his ministry until he attended a lecture by Dr. Mordecai W. Johnson, president of Howard University. Martin heard the speech in Philadelphia, PA while he was a student at Crozer Seminary. Dr. Johnson's lecture was about the life of a social and political leader named Mahatma Gandhi, a man who led the people of India in nonviolent protests against the British government, which ruled that country until 1947.

Gandhi was a small, thin man who wore eyeglasses and clothed his body in white linen. But he became a powerful figure by spreading his belief that freedom and social justice could be won in India using love, self-sacrifice, and truth as weapons.

Coretta wrote that Martin was so moved by Gandhi's philosophy that he read every book he could find on the subject and immersed himself in Gandhi's doctrine of *satyagraha* ("holding onto truth"), the belief that government oppression could be stopped by nonviolent citizen boycotts, strikes, and marches. Satyagraha complemented Martin's belief in Christianity and in Jesus' peaceful example of facing evil and overcoming enemies.

Martin didn't know exactly what he would do after he completed his Ph.D. studies, but he felt a

Martin (front row, fourth from left) experienced a very different childhood from that of Coretta. Here he is shown attending a birthday party at age six with friends from his solidly middle-class Atlanta neighborhood.

deep desire to use his gifts to serve God. He also knew he didn't want to fulfill his life's mission alone: Martin longed for a wife and family.

To that end, it didn't take long for Martin to call Coretta after their first date. He suggested that they get together that Saturday night. But Coretta already had plans; furthermore, she already had a date for the small party she was scheduled to attend. Coretta told Martin that he was welcome to come with her if her escort could not make it. Undeterred, Martin kept his calendar open.

As luck would have it, Coretta did go to the party on the arm of Martin Luther King Jr. Other young women at the party fawned over her date, but she pretended to be oblivious to their fussing—and to Martin's pleasure in it.

But Martin was smitten. The young couple shared long walks and conversations and socialized with friends at small dinner parties. They also went dancing and even attended a piano concert together.

Soon, Martin's intention to marry Coretta was unmistakably clear. But there was one problem: he was already engaged to a young woman in Atlanta. The engagement had been informally set up by the couple's respective families with Martin Sr.'s approval. Martin had little interest in marrying a woman who was handpicked for him, but he also had a difficult time defying his father's wishes.

Coretta knew about the engagement and Martin's reluctance to approach his father. She wasn't in a hurry to decide her fate, anyway. Coretta desperately wanted to continue her studies; she also still preferred to marry someone other than a minister. Martin greatly admired Coretta's musical talent and her intellectual pursuits, but he made it clear that he wanted a mate who would be a wife and a mother.

By the summer of 1952, Coretta had made some hard decisions about her role in the relationship. She had grown to love Martin. When her sister

Edythe came to Boston to meet him, she gave Coretta the nod of approval. In fact, Edythe eventually helped Coretta make up her mind about Martin, telling her that, although she might not have the career she had so long envisioned, she would certainly not be without a career if she married him. But Coretta was determined to complete her studies at the conservatory, regardless of Martin's intentions.

During the summer, Coretta visited Atlanta to meet the King family. Reverend and Mrs. King were polite, but they didn't make any grand overtures to their son's new love interest. After all, Martin was still "engaged." Coretta took the tension in stride. She visited Ebenezer Church and stayed with Mary Powell's family.

That fall, the Kings came to Boston. Daddy King insisted that his son reconsider his fiancée in Atlanta. Coretta listened politely as Martin Sr. listed the fine points of all of the Atlanta girls that Martin had chosen to ignore thus far. Her patience flagging, she finally looked at Daddy King, unafraid, and said, "I have something to offer too."

Soon after—perhaps buoyed by the courage of his intended—Martin told his father that he planned to finish his doctoral studies in Boston and marry Coretta Scott. By Christmas, the Kings were convinced that Martin and Coretta would be husband and wife. Daddy King finally gave his blessing.

Coretta told her family the good news and began to make wedding plans. She decided to change her major at the conservatory to music education and voice. This degree would enable her to teach for a living as well as to perform professionally.

Coretta Scott and Martin Luther King Jr. were married on June 18, 1953, on the lawn of the Scott family's new home. Obadiah had built the house fairly recently, next to his general store in Marion. Martin Sr. performed the wedding ceremony. At the

Martin Luther King Sr. preaches at Ebenezer Baptist Church. When Martin was 18, Daddy King made him assistant pastor at Ebenezer. Twelve years later, father and son would be co-pastors of the same church after Martin returned to Atlanta.

request of his son and daughter-in-law, Daddy King omitted the bride's vow to "obey" her husband.

The newlyweds spent their honeymoon in Alabama at the home of a family friend who owned a funeral parlor. The young couple had no other choice because blacks were not allowed to stay at white-owned hotels or motels. Although the reasons behind their somewhat strange choice of bridal suite were painful, the couple's honeymoon in a funeral parlor eventually became a source of gentle joking by Martin.

The Monday after her wedding, Coretta took a summer job in Atlanta clerking for a bank that Daddy King helped run. She and Martin stayed with the Kings until fall, when they returned to Boston to complete their degrees. Coretta crammed her schedule with 13 courses—voice lessons and lessons in playing several new instruments. She also worked in another student-teaching program and performed in several recitals.

Martin worked on finishing his doctoral thesis. During their first year of marriage, Coretta and Martin shared household chores, cooking, and grocery shopping because her course load was so heavy. Martin made it clear that he was the head of the household, though. Coretta wrote about one notable instance of Martin asserting his authority. On this occasion, her young husband said, "I want my wife to respect me as the head of the family. I am the head of the family."

Coretta wrote, "We laughed together at that slightly pompous speech, and he backed down. 'Of course, I don't really mean that,' he said. 'I think marriage should be a shared partnership.'"

But Coretta was insightful enough to know that part of Martin really did mean it, and that she would have to make adjustments to married life. She felt strongly that it was important to retain some independence, and she still hoped someday to perform as a singer in a professional setting. In the years to come, Coretta would nurture her family while also using her creative talents outside the home as a singer and a teacher. To support his wife's aspirations, Martin would later purchase a piano for her so that she could continue playing.

While the couple lived in Boston, Martin preached at local churches to help pay expenses. This experience led Martin to think about beginning a ministry in the South. "I preach because I can't help myself," he told Coretta.

Coretta could not have foreseen the changes that would come as a result of her husband's seemingly simple dream.

5

THE WINDS OF CHANGE

The South's racially unjust traditions and laws were held up to public scrutiny in the spring of 1954. On May 17, the United States Supreme Court, ruling on a case called *Brown v. Board of Education*, declared that educational facilities that kept blacks separate from whites were "inherently unequal." The court's decision meant that the federal government could no longer sanction the legal separation of blacks and whites in public schools. In 1955, the Court ordered the states to desegregate their public education systems "with all deliberate speed."

The tradition that Coretta, Martin, and thousands of other southern blacks grew up with—separate schools—was now illegal. The court's decision was the first step in ending racial segregation in the South and throughout the country.

Brown v. Board of Education was a victory for southern blacks. The NAACP Legal Defense and Education Fund had tried for more than 10 years to convince southern courts that laws permitting the separation of blacks from whites in public life were against the legal and moral principles of the 14th amendment to the U.S. Constitution, which guarantees all Americans equal protection under the law, regardless of race. Thurgood Marshall, a brilliant black lawyer and director of the NAACP

Coretta, Martin, and two unidentified men leave the Montgomery courthouse during the 1956 bus boycott. Their leadership of the boycott thrust the young couple—who were also new parents at the time—into the national news.

Even before Brown v. Board of Education *in 1954, Thurgood Marshall (left) was fighting to desegregate educational facilities. Here he works with Charles Houston (right) and Donald Gaines Murray (center) on a 1935 lawsuit against the University of Maryland.* Brown v. Board of Education *heartened Coretta and Martin, but it also made them less willing to tolerate racism in other areas of public life.*

Legal Defense Fund, led the battle against segregation in public schools and won. It finally seemed as if African Americans could rely upon the highest court in the land to guarantee and defend their rights.

For Coretta and Martin, the legal end of segregation coincided with a new beginning in one of the most racially divided cities in the nation—Montgomery, Alabama. During the Civil War, Montgomery had been known as "The Cradle of the Confederacy"; as late as the 1950s, blacks and whites could be arrested for socializing together in public.

Martin was offered the pastoral seat at Dexter Avenue Baptist Church in Montgomery; he couldn't refuse the challenge. Dexter was the home church of a middle-class congregation that had grown apathetic in the face of racial injustices. Martin hoped he could inspire the congregants to work for social justice on behalf of the entire black community. If he could motivate the people, he could then put his beliefs about nonviolence and social justice into practice.

Martin officially began his ministry on September 1, 1954. Coretta, who graduated from the New England Conservatory that June, had serious reservations about returning to the South. "I wanted to breathe the freer air and the richer cultural life of the north a while longer and to enjoy the greater opportunities a northern city would give me for furthering my musical career," she recalled in her autobiography. A major legal milestone may have been won against segregation, but racism was still a fact of life in the South.

But Martin felt an urgent need to pastor at a southern black church, so Coretta made up her mind to make the best of the situation. She quickly made friends with Juanita Abernathy, the wife of Ralph Abernathy, a young and outspoken black minister who pastored at the First Baptist Church, also in Montgomery. Like Martin, Abernathy believed the Christian gospel was an instrument for social change. The two men also enjoyed poking fun at each other.

This was fortunate, because Martin needed a strong sense of humor to weather his first year at Dexter. Balancing his ministry with the rest of his life was a logistical challenge: he preached every Sunday, wrote all of his sermons, and traveled back and forth to Boston to finish his thesis. To set an example for his congregants, Martin also joined the local chapter of the NAACP and the Alabama Council on Human Relations, an interracial civic group in the city.

Coretta was also very busy. Martin considered her his best critic and often turned to her for sermon ideas before putting pen to paper. Her musical gifts and training served her well as a soloist and helper in Dexter Avenue Baptist's choir. A few months after settling in Montgomery, she also performed in a concert in Georgia. In early 1955, she sang in two concerts, but stopped performing that spring after discovering that she was pregnant. The couple was ecstatic to learn they were going to be parents. In June, Martin was awarded his Ph.D. from Boston University.

Coretta gave birth to her first child, Yolanda Denise (Yoki) on November 17, 1955. She came home from the hospital a week after the baby was born, hoping to get acclimated to motherhood in peace. But the winds of change began to blow in the South with great urgency just weeks after Yoki's birth.

Rosa Parks, a 42-year-old seamstress at a local department store, was riding a city bus home from work one day when she decided not to relinquish her seat to a white passenger. At the time, blacks were required to sit in the back of the bus, while whites sat in the front. If no seats were available in the black section, black passengers had to stand— regardless of how many empty seats were in the white section.

But on December 1, 1955, the bus was so crowd- ed that no seats went unoccupied. At each bus stop, more white passengers boarded and demanded that black riders yield their seats. But Rosa Parks wasn't moving an inch. The bus driver told her to give up her seat or be arrested, but Parks refused. She was apprehended by police and taken to city hall.

News of her arrest spread through the black community like wildfire. Historian David Garrow writes in his book *Bearing the Cross* that E. D. Dixon, a former president of the local NAACP, called Ralph Abernathy about Parks's arrest. According to Garrow, Dixon and Jo Ann Robinson, president of the Women's Political Council (WPC), decided to organize a black boycott of Montgomery buses to protest the arrest and to push political leaders to make the city's segregation laws more equitable. Black passengers had endured years of harassment by white bus drivers and passengers alike, and they could be jailed for not giving up their seats to whites. Dixon wanted to arrange a meeting of black leaders to organize the boycott, and Abernathy suggested Martin Luther King Jr. to spearhead it.

Martin agreed to hold a meeting of black religious and civic leaders at Dexter church on Friday, December 2. More than 40 people showed up. They discussed the situation at length and finally decided to hold the boycott the following Monday, December 5—the day of Mrs. Parks's trial.

King and the other leaders spent that weekend preparing their communities for the boycott. More than 50,000 blacks lived in Montgomery, so there was a lot of work to do. The organizers distributed leaflets explaining the importance of the boycott. Black-owned taxi companies were asked to provide group rates for blacks who were commuting to and from work. Everyone in the community was urged to stay off the city buses. Coretta manned the phone all weekend, taking calls from community leaders and citizens who wanted updates and help coordinating volunteer car pools.

The Sunday night before the boycott was scheduled to begin, Coretta had planned to retire early. But between her crying infant and the ringing telephone, it was not to be. Instead, she stayed up until after midnight discussing the likelihood of the protest's success with Martin. The South Jackson Avenue bus stop—part of the busiest line in the city—was on the corner outside the King home, so Martin and Coretta would get a close look the results of all of their hard work when the first bus of the day arrived at 6:00 A.M. on Monday.

Coretta was up and dressed by 5:30 the next morning, eager to see the boycott in action. She and

Martin had toast and coffee as they awaited the 6:00 bus. It arrived on schedule, and Coretta was ready to greet it. The bus was empty! Not one passenger was on board. Coretta called Martin to the window as the bus rolled away. They went outside to await the next one; it was also empty, as were several others that followed.

Similar scenes were taking place throughout the city. Boycotters walked, rode in taxis, or pedaled bicycles; they simply found other ways to get to and from work. A few mules and horse-drawn buggies were also seen plodding along the streets of Montgomery. The city's black residents were determined make their discontent known.

At 9:00 A.M. Martin and Abernathy arrived at the city courthouse for Mrs. Parks's trial. The judge ruled that she had violated a state segregation law and fined her $10. When her lawyer, Fred D. Gray, filed an appeal, the legal battle over Montgomery's segregation laws was under way.

Later that day, black community leaders met to form an organization that would lead and sustain the bus boycott until the segregation law was defeated. Abernathy suggested that the group be called the Montgomery Improvement Association (MIA). Martin reluctantly accepted the president's post, unsure whether he was the right person to lead the group. After all, he already had his hands full pastoring at Dexter and taking care of his family. Even more worrisome was the potential danger to himself, Coretta, and Yoki that leadership of a civil-rights group would entail in such a racist climate. But Coretta supported his decision, saying, "You know that whatever you do, you have my backing."

More than 1,000 supporters came to the Holy Baptist Church to hear a speech by the new leader of the boycott movement. Although he was nervous, Martin later told Coretta that God had carried him through his largely extemporaneous speech, made before a cheering crowd.

"There comes a time when people get tired; tired of being segregated and humiliated; tired of being kicked around," Martin proclaimed to the crowd. He insisted that the boycott was a tool to win justice without violence. "Our actions must be guided by the deepest principles of Christian faith," he said, asking the boycotters not to hate their white neighbors. Martin called upon the people to find the faith and the courage to protest with dignity. "This is our charge," he said, "our overwhelming responsibility."

The audience's response was immediate—everyone jumped to their feet and cheered. The black community pledged to support the MIA's three demands: that the harassment of black bus passengers was to end; that bus companies were to adopt a first-come, first-served seating policy, with blacks taking seats from the back of the bus forward, and whites from the front moving backward; and that black bus drivers were to be hired to drive city bus routes that served black neighborhoods.

Martin and the other MIA leaders worked to negotiate an agreement to desegregate the buses with city officials and the bus companies, but the bus companies refused to bargain, so the boycott continued. By mid-December, the MIA had to organize numerous volunteer car pools to take blacks to and from work. The King home became MIA headquarters and Coretta played an important role. She answered telephone calls, coordinated car pools, and updated boycotters on the ongoing schedule of community meetings. All the while, Coretta cooked for her husband and his colleagues whenever they met at the King home, and cared for Yoki, who was only a few weeks old.

The protesters were well organized and strong-willed. The MIA held meetings at black churches throughout the city twice a week to encourage and

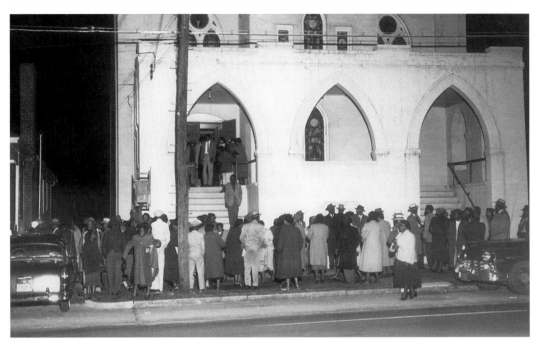

A mass meeting at the St. John's A.M.E. Church on February 21, 1956. The city's long bus boycott was sustained by members of Montgomery's black clergy, who hosted mass meetings in their churches to boost morale in the face of arrests, fines, and the threat of violence.

inspire the people. Martin continued to preach his message of nonviolent resistance, urging blacks not to give up their rights—but not to hate, either.

Many whites were furious at the success of the boycott. Martin's doctrine of nonviolence and love was considered a declaration of war on white supremacy. Racist whites resented Martin's leadership. He was young, intelligent, educated, articulate, well-mannered, and blessed with a lovely wife and a healthy newborn. To many whites, Dr. Martin Luther King Jr. was an "uppity" black who needed to be taken down.

In January of 1956, Coretta and Martin began to receive obscene and threatening phone calls. The White Citizens Council—a group that historians call the "white-collar Ku Klux Klan"—watched the King family very closely. Important city officials were rumored to be members of the council.

Coretta was deeply offended by the calls, but also inconvenienced; she had to use the phone in her work for the MIA. One day, 30 to 40 disturbing phone calls were made to the Kings' home. Coretta soon found it necessary to take the phone off the hook for several hours each night.

But the couple's concern about the calls paled in comparison with their fear of being bombed. Other bombings had occurred in rural areas outside the city; even though he and Coretta lived in a densely populated area, Martin still feared that their home might be targeted. But Coretta told Martin, "I'm not afraid to be alone," when members of their congregation worried about her safety in his absence.

On January 10, 1956, the Kings' worst nightmare came true. While Martin was giving an MIA speech at Abernathy's church, Coretta and Mary Lucy Williams, a friend from Dexter Avenue Church, heard a loud thump on the porch of the Kings' home. It was 9:30 P.M.

Coretta, mentally prepared for the possibility of an attack, reacted swiftly. "It sounds as if someone has hit the house. We'd better move to the back," she instructed her terrified friend.

Dressed in her bathrobe, Coretta led Mary Lucy Williams to the back bedroom where Yoki was lying in her bassinet. The women heard a blast that shook the house and filled the air with smoke.

After making sure that her daughter was unharmed, Coretta grabbed the telephone. Then, as she recalled in her autobiography, she suddenly felt uneasy about calling the police. She called the church where her husband was speaking instead. Martin rushed home to find the living room windows smashed, the porch split in half, and all of the house lights blown out.

But his family was safe. "Thank God you and the baby are all right!" Martin exclaimed, kissing Coretta. Then, noticing that his wife was walking around in her bathrobe, Martin calmly suggested that she get dressed.

The Kings' neighbors had long since gathered at

the house to see if they could help. The mayor and the police commissioner also came. Several black neighbors, outraged and anxious to retaliate for the bombing, clashed with police officers who were on the scene. It was Martin who defused this potentially explosive situation, exhorting his supporters to "meet violence with nonviolence." The mayor and police commissioner offered a $5,000 reward for information identifying the bomber, but many of Martin's supporters took this show of official support with a grain of salt as they turned to go home.

The bombing did not break the King family's resolve to lead the boycott. Shortly after the explosion, Obadiah came to collect his daughter and granddaughter and take them to safety in Marion. But Coretta declined, saying, "I would not be satisfied if I went home. I want to be here with Martin." Daddy King made his own desperate bid to get the young family to return with him to Atlanta. But Coretta and Martin were determined to stay put. They returned to their house in Montgomery as soon as it was repaired, and made adjustments in their lives to protect themselves and Yoki. These measures included an unarmed night watchman and outside floodlights.

"Coretta, you've been a real soldier," Martin told his wife. "I don't know what I would have done if it had not been for you."

Martin's praise affected her deeply. "I had always been a strong person," she later wrote, "but I had not realized that Martin, so strong himself, did need me."

Several days after the bombing, Coretta silently reflected upon the sudden threat to her family's life. She found the experience surprisingly enlightening. Coretta finally realized why she had married Martin. "I felt there was a larger force working with me and that I was not alone," Coretta recalled years later. "I knew at that point that being with him, and participating in the Movement, was the right thing

for me." Coretta's hopes of returning to the North were replaced by a deep commitment to the fight against social injustice. She would never again question her mission in life.

After three months, the boycott was still going strong, and city officials fumed. To topple it, the city found an obscure law against boycotting on its books, then charged about 90 of the bus protest's leaders with a violation. Martin, who was on a lecture tour when the arrests began, canceled his speaking engagements and hurried to Atlanta, where Coretta and Yoki were visiting with Mamma and Daddy King. Martin knew he would be arrested immediately upon returning to Montgomery. Still,

Coretta accompanies Martin to the Montgomery courthouse for his conspiracy trial in March 1956. He was the prime target of city officials who, in an effort to break the bus boycott, charged about 90 of its leaders with violating an obscure law against such protests.

his resolve to go back was not shaken, even after Daddy King tearfully begged him to stay in Atlanta. Coretta weighed in with her own opinion during this tense time, her newfound sense of purpose resonating in every word:

> Martin, there comes a time in every person's life when he has to make a decision all by himself, when he has to stand alone. This is such a time in your life. You know that what you feel is right, and I want you to know that whatever you decide to do, I will always be with you.

The next morning, Martin turned himself in at the Montgomery courthouse, accompanied by Ralph Abernathy (who had already been arrested and released on bail) and Daddy King. His trial began on March 19, 1956. The judge found him guilty and sentenced him to pay $500 or serve 386 days of hard labor. Martin's lawyers appealed the decision.

The wheels of justice had been grinding for months in the lawsuit that the MIA leaders had filed after the arrest of Rosa Parks. The MIA hoped to question the legality of Alabama's segregation laws. In June, a federal court ruled that the laws were unconstitutional, but the city's lawyers appealed the case to the Supreme Court. All the boycotters could do was continue to protest—and wait.

By this time, Martin Luther King was becoming a national figure, even a household name. Newspaper and television reporters from around the country traveled to Alabama to cover the pending appeal, and black and liberal leaders from both the South and the North began to wonder about the MIA and its president. Bayard Rustin, a civil rights and peace activist who had traveled to India many years before to study Gandhi's nonviolent movement, came to Montgomery to help the MIA map out strategies to sustain the boycott.

Coretta had heard Rustin speak about his trip to India when she was a student at Lincoln High School. She had heard one of his lectures again while at Antioch.

Stanley Levison, a white attorney, served as legal counsel for the MIA. Both Levison and Rustin were members of a New York organization called In Friendship that raised money to help poor southerners fight legal battles.

The boycott continued through the fall, but by then black participants were being harassed more than ever. Boycotters were pulled out of cars and beaten. Black-owned gas stations were bombed, further hampering the car pools. Even walking to work involved a high risk of bodily harm for the protesters. It was becoming more difficult for the leaders to maintain their morale. Coretta continued to coordinate the boycott from the Kings' home, but

Martin (back seat, left) rode the first desegregated Montgomery city bus on the morning of December 21, 1956. Ralph Abernathy (left), Rosa Parks, and New York minister Glenn Smiley (not shown) joined him that day in demonstrating the boycott's triumphant outcome.

the project was losing steam.

In late October of 1956, the Montgomery city government went to court to get an injunction to stop carpooling in black communities. The city claimed the car pools were a "public nuisance" which compromised the quality of life in the city. The boycott was now in serious danger.

A court hearing for November 13 was scheduled to settle the matter. Martin and the other black leaders were worried. The Sunday before the hearing, Martin urged his congregants not to give up hope and to keep their faith in God. But this time, it was hard for the protesters not to imagine the worst.

Martin confided his worries to Coretta. She tried to reassure him, telling him, "You know, what I think is going to happen is that by the time they get this injunction, the Supreme Court will have ruled for us. I think everything is going to work out all right."

Coretta later admitted in her autobiography that she wasn't even sure she believed this optimistic forecast herself.

But she need not have worried. While sitting in the courtroom, Martin was handed an urgent message from a reporter. It said that the Supreme Court had ruled Alabama's state and local laws requiring segregation of buses unconstitutional. The legal battle that had begun with Rosa Parks was finally over. Racial segregation on city buses was now illegal; the MIA and the boycotters had won.

Coretta celebrated the historic occasion in a very special way. On December 5, 1956, the first anniversary of the boycott, she performed in a concert at the Manhattan Center in New York to raise funds for the MIA. The featured act on a list that included such luminaries as Duke Ellington and Harry Belafonte (who became a close family friend), Coretta sang a program of classical music and an original composition that told the story of the bus boycott. She had interwoven spoken narrative with gospel songs to convey the struggle for freedom throughout history.

Coretta was jubilant that night. "I could feel the warm responsive love between us," she later wrote, describing the bond she forged with her audience. This was one time Coretta was glad she never gave up on her dream to become a concert singer.

On December 20, a long-awaited dream of Montgomery's black community also came true. The U.S. Supreme Court ruling to desegregate the city's buses went into effect. The mayor declared that the bus companies would obey the ruling and that the police would cooperate.

The next morning, Rosa Parks joined Martin, Ralph Abernathy, and MIA treasurer E. D. Nixon on a ride aboard the first desegregated bus on the South Jackson Avenue line. After 382 long days of nonviolent protest, change was slowly coming to Montgomery, Alabama. Coretta and Martin knew that there could be no turning back in the fight for civil rights.

6

FOR BETTER OR WORSE

❦

Coretta juggled her roles as mother, wife, and de facto secretary of the Montgomery Improvement Association with grace and steely determination. So much work had to be done—taking care of Yoki, keeping her home intact, participating in her husband's work, and maintaining her musical skills—that it seemed there weren't enough hours in the day to sit back and reflect on how her life was changing.

Coretta was now the wife of the most newsworthy black leader in America. People—both black and white—wanted to know more about the dynamic young southern preacher who was turning the racist South upside down with a fervent nonviolent protest movement. The MIA maintained contact with scores of newspaper reporters who came to Montgomery to record the ongoing events.

Black ministers throughout the South began to follow the MIA's example, organizing their congregations to fight racial injustice. Bayard Rustin convinced Martin it was time to bring all the emerging church protest groups under one national organization that would use nonviolence to promote social, political, and economic equity for southern blacks. Daddy King agreed to hold a meeting of black leaders at his church in Atlanta. Fred Shuttlesworth, a black minister and president of the

Martin's frequent arrests forced Coretta to come to terms with the possibility of his being harmed. In this photo, she greets him at a Georgia airport after his particularly harrowing incarceration at Reidsville Prison.

Alabama Christian Movement for Human Rights in Montgomery, helped Martin organize the meeting, which was scheduled to take place January 10 and 11, 1957, at Ebenezer Baptist Church in Atlanta.

But the night before the meeting was supposed to convene, Montgomery's black community was besieged by a sudden rash of church firebombings. Ralph Abernathy's church was partially destroyed. Martin asked Coretta to take his place at the meeting so that he and Abernathy could return to Montgomery to help the community cope with the tragic violence.

Coretta was the meeting's first speaker. She notified the assembly of the bombings in Montgomery and presented the MIA's plan for building a southern coalition to direct the protest movement. The gathering of ministers and civic leaders unanimously supported the plan. Martin returned to Atlanta for the second day of meetings, where it was decided that there would be a larger follow-up meeting in New Orleans.

The Southern Christian Leadership Conference (SCLC) was born at that meeting on February 14, 1957. The organization's headquarters was established in Atlanta. Martin was elected president.

Ella Baker, a smart, strong-willed, and outspoken grassroots activist who worked with the NAACP and the In Friendship group in New York, became the SCLC's executive secretary. She was responsible for running the SCLC office and taking care of the organization's day-to-day activities. Years later, she would advise Coretta on how to be more fully involved in the movement.

As soon as the SCLC was established, Martin sent President Dwight Eisenhower the second of two messages from the organization asking him to investigate racial injustice in the South and to respond to the terrorist attacks that had followed the Montgomery boycott. Unfortunately, the White

House remained silent.

On February 18, Martin's photograph appeared on the cover of *Time* magazine. The story highlighted Martin's leadership during the Montgomery boycott.

In the spring, Coretta and Martin traveled to the West African nation of Ghana to attend that country's Independence Day celebration. They also visited France, Italy, Britain and Switzerland. Martin began to travel more frequently both in America and abroad, lecturing for universities and civic organizations. He talked about the importance of nonviolence and encouraged people of all races to work together for social justice.

Meanwhile, the SCLC learned that President Eisenhower had been quietly trying to push a major

Coretta poses with Martin and Mama King (left) at a press conference held during his recuperation from a near-fatal stabbing in September 1958. Neither Martin nor Coretta harbored any ill feelings toward his assailant, a mentally ill black woman who plunged a letter opener into his chest.

civil rights bill through Congress. The proposed legislation would give the federal government the power to investigate civil rights violations against blacks and to intercede on behalf of blacks who were denied the right to vote.

The legislation was extremely important; a major civil rights law had not been passed in the United States since the 1800s. Black men had been granted the right to vote with the passage of the 15th Amendment in 1870, but since that time, laws called "grandfather clauses" had prevented many southern blacks from exercising their right. Grandfather clauses prohibited blacks from voting if their grandfathers—who had been slaves—could not register to do so. Poll taxes also kept blacks away from the ballot box. Most southern states had laws requiring blacks to pay as much as two dollars to vote, plus back taxes for every year they had not voted since age 21. None of these restrictions applied to whites. They were designed to prevent poor, undereducated blacks from exercising their rights as citizens.

When Martin returned from his travels abroad, he spent most of his time helping the SCLC organize a Prayer Pilgrimage for Freedom in support of the president's pending voting rights bill. Martin was busy, but he was also thrilled with his growing family: Coretta was pregnant with their second child.

On May 17, 1957, more than 30,000 people marched to the steps of the Lincoln Memorial to hear Martin Luther King Jr. outline the SCLC's next move against racial discrimination in the South. "Give us the ballot," Martin said to the thousands of supporters who traveled to Washington, D.C., for the Prayer Pilgrimage. "[W]e will transform the salient misdeeds of the blood-thirsty mobs into the calculated good deeds of orderly citizens!"

After the pilgrimage, the SCLC began plans to

launch a massive voter education and registration drive throughout the South. The organization hoped to register 5 million new black voters. In all the southern states, only 1.25 million blacks were registered.

Martin and Coretta were a busy couple. Martin continued with his pastoral duties at Dexter and traveled, giving speeches and lectures. He was not home much: as a matter of fact, an article in *Jet* magazine estimated that he gave more than 200 speeches and traveled 780,000 miles in one year.

When he was at home, Martin spent his time finishing the last chapters of *Stride Toward Freedom*, his first book. In it, he told the story of the Montgomery bus boycott. On October 23, 1957, Coretta gave birth to Martin Luther King III, the King family's first son. With his birth, Coretta's responsibilities multiplied, but she still juggled everything in her life with grace and efficiency.

In the spring of 1958, Coretta packed her bags and hit the road to make her debut as a public speaker. The New Hope Baptist Church in Denver had invited her to be the guest speaker for its Women's Day program. Coretta shared the Kings' experiences during the boycott and discussed the growing nonviolent protest movement begun by the SCLC. She also performed selections from the Freedom Concert program that she had premiered two years earlier in New York City.

On September 17, *Stride Toward Freedom* was published, and a national book tour followed. Martin flew to New York for a book signing while Coretta stayed home with the children. Two days later, she was expecting Martin to arrive home. But when the phone rang on the night of September 19, Coretta received shocking news. Dr. O. Clay Maxwell, a Baptist minister and friend from New York City, told her that Martin had been stabbed during a book signing at a department

By 1960, Coretta and Martin had survived a bombing, an assassination attempt, and numerous death threats for their unflinching belief in equality for all people. Martin, holding Martin III, studies a cross burned during the previous night on his front lawn in Atlanta.

store in Harlem. He had been rushed to Harlem Hospital for surgery.

"He's alive," the minister said, "but it is serious, very serious."

Coretta informed her brother Obie, who was visiting from Marion, what had happened. When Ralph Abernathy called to confirm the news, Coretta's sobs punctuated the conversation. Abernathy agreed to travel to New York with her and Christine, Martin's sister.

"All the hours I was enroute, I kept thinking about the possibility of Martin's death," Coretta wrote years after the event. "At the same time I tried to tell myself that he would survive."

Martin was lucky. He had been stabbed with a

letter opener; the blade had come to rest against his aorta. Had the blade sliced this juncture of arteries, Martin would have bled to death. When Coretta arrived at her husband's hospital room, he was barely conscious, but their eyes met. Looking at her fragile husband, Coretta silently came to terms with the fact that Martin could be killed at any time. His work in the nonviolent protest movement made him a marked man. The threat was most worrisome in the South, where many whites seethed with resentment over his attempts to bring about racial justice. But this attack had come in Harlem, and the assailant, Mrs. Isola Curry, was a mentally unstable black woman.

Coretta's faith was challenged in a way it had never been before. Could she continue at her husband's side, withstanding the constant threat of danger, without bitterness toward his enemies?

By the first Sunday in December, Martin had fully recovered. He returned to the pulpit at the Dexter Avenue Baptist Church and delivered a sermon that reminded his congregation to be thankful for the blessings of the holiday season. This was one Christmas that Martin and Coretta were especially grateful to see.

Early in the following year, the Kings traveled to India. Martin explored the homeland of Gandhi, his spiritual mentor, learning more about the leader's philosophy and teachings. He had a lengthy visit with Jawaharlal Nehru, India's prime minister, discussing Gandhi's protest movement and the effectiveness of nonviolent activism. Martin's work with the SCLC was progressing slowly—President Eisenhower's long-awaited voting rights law was deadlocked in Congress—and he hoped the trip would give him new insights on how to push the civil rights agenda forward.

Coretta was busy performing Freedom Concerts throughout India to educate that country's people about the black struggle for social justice in America.

Coretta and Martin returned to Montgomery with a renewed dedication to the principles of nonviolence and a new commitment to the SCLC's voter registration drive. The Kings decided to move to Atlanta so Martin could be closer to the organization's main headquarters. Martin passed on his duties as president of the MIA to Abernathy, and with Daddy King's help, he returned to the spiritual home of his childhood and was named his father's co-pastor at the Ebenezer Baptist Church in February 1960. The family moved into a modest house a few blocks away from the church.

As soon as the Kings were settled, Coretta joined the local branch of the Women's International League for Peace and Freedom, which worked to stop nuclear proliferation by convincing world leaders to outlaw the testing of atomic weapons. Coretta was proud to join the group. She knew any contribution she made to the world's peace movement also would aid the black civil-rights struggle by helping to unite all people.

She also found her family's mettle tested yet again soon after settling in Atlanta. Martin was indicted by the state of Alabama for allegedly falsifying his income tax returns for 1956 and 1958; the charges implied that he had pocketed income from the MIA and the SCLC by not recording it properly. Coretta was saddened to see that this attack on his integrity was even harder on Martin than the physical assault he had endured the year before.

To Coretta's astonishment, a jury of 12 white men from Montgomery acquitted Martin on May 28, 1960. But then she faced another hurdle: she was scheduled to speak at three separate church services the next day for Women's Day at Antioch Baptist Church. Coretta left directly from the trial for Cleveland, arriving at 5:00 A.M. Her first speech was scheduled for 11:00, and she had not had any time to prepare a presentation.

Ralph Abernathy, who had accompanied her, said, "Coretta, I think you ought to speak about your experience this week; just talk about that."

She did just that for 40 minutes after she was introduced that morning. Speaking extemporaneously about "those long days in court, the terrible anxiety, and the triumphant conclusion," Coretta captured and held her audience's attention. Their enthusiastic response afterward confirmed her success. Martin was not the only member of the family who possessed a gift for oratory.

Around this time, black college students began to heed the call for nonviolent protests against social injustice. In April 1960, more than 350 students from colleges throughout the South had met at Shaw University in Raleigh, North Carolina, to form a youth organization to coordinate mass protests. Black students had held a series of sit-ins at department store lunch counters to demand that black customers be served. During these sit-ins, students sat in silence and refused to move for white customers. The sit-in movement was spreading to cities in North Carolina, Virginia, and Florida, and it needed a national group to keep people's passions alive.

The Student Nonviolent Coordinating Committee (SNCC) was born at Shaw University, and Martin and Ella Baker agreed to serve as the group's advisors. The SCLC provided office space and funding for the students.

In October, Martin and a group of 75 black students and civic leaders staged a sit-in at Rich's Department Store in Atlanta. The protesters agreed not to pay bail if they were arrested. More than 30 people, including Martin, were taken to Atlanta's Fulton County jail.

Five days later, the mayor released all of the sit-in protesters except Martin. He was taken to a jail

Black protesters stage a sit-in at an Atlanta lunch counter in 1960. Martin advocated sit-ins as a nonviolent method of convincing white retailers to provide blacks with both service and job opportunities.

in Dekalb County—the reputed headquarters of the Ku Klux Klan. Martin was cleared of charges relating to the sit-in, but police in DeKalb County held him on an old probation violation that stemmed from an invalid driver's license.

The judge sentenced Martin to six months of hard labor at the State Penitentiary in Reidsville. Coretta was five months pregnant with the Kings' third child. When she heard the sentence, she broke down. It was the first—and only—time Coretta wept in public. Daddy King admonished her to stop crying, but it was no use. Coretta's spirit was momentarily broken. The Reidsville prison was 300 miles away from Atlanta. Coretta worried that she could not make the long trip until after she had delivered, and she wondered how her young family would cope with the long separation.

Martin was taken from the court in handcuffs

and put back into a cell. "Corrie, dear, you have to be strong," he told her when she and Daddy King came to see him. Daddy King, hiding his own anguish, also rallied his daughter-in-law. "You don't see me crying; I am ready to fight. When you see Daddy crying, Coretta, then you can start crying. I'm not taking this lying down."

Coretta regained her composure, but she still had grave worries about Martin's safety. Her worries were exacerbated when she learned the next morning that Martin had been transferred to Reidsville under cover of darkness.

News of Martin's arrest flooded the nation's airwaves. Reporters called the SCLC for updates on Martin's condition. Daddy King, SCLC associates, and lawyers worked feverishly to get Martin out of jail.

As Daddy King worked the legal system to regain his son's freedom, Senator John F. Kennedy, a Democratic candidate in the 1960 presidential election, gave Coretta an unexpected phone call. He told her he was concerned about Martin and his family. He offered to help in any way he could; Coretta thankfully accepted.

Senator Kennedy stood by his word. Kennedy's campaign manager and younger brother, Robert, called the judge in Martin's case. Before Coretta knew it, her fears were laid to rest. Martin was released from prison on a $2,000 bond. The SCLC flew him home to Atlanta. Later that fall, Senator John F. Kennedy won the presidential election by a slim margin—a margin that Coretta later attributed to his intervention on behalf of Martin.

On January 30, 1961, Coretta gave birth to her third child, Dexter Scott King. Thanks to his many supporters, Martin was free to share in this happy event.

7
BIRMINGHAM

❦

In March 1962, Coretta was one of a group of 50 American women who traveled to Geneva, Switzerland, in an effort to establish an international ban on the testing of all atomic weapons. The trip was sponsored by the Women Strike for Peace, and Coretta was honored when she received the invitation to go.

Coretta and three other black women were part of the delegation, which met with women from Scandinavia, Britain, the U.S.S.R., and Australia. On the plane to Geneva, Coretta found her fellow delegates to be "very stable, intelligent, and level-headed." She was very much at home in the company of so many bright and politically active women.

But the trip to Geneva proved disappointing. The American women's delegation was brushed off by Arthur Dean, the United States representative at the conference. Coretta wrote years later that she felt that Dean perceived the delegation as a group of "hysterical" women, rather than a serious organization of concerned citizens. The meeting ended abruptly when the women were curtly advised by Dean to consult the Soviet government.

The women did just that. The Soviets discussed nuclear testing with them in an open manner, and even held a reception to honor them. Although impressed by the cordial treatment the women

When Coretta received a call from President Kennedy during her husband's imprisonment in Birmingham, she made sure that the SCLC's leaders alerted the media. Birmingham officials responded by releasing King and Ralph Abernathy from jail.

87

received from the Soviets, Coretta realized that "the Russians were masters of the art of propaganda," and would as a matter of course treat them well to elicit a positive response. But once back on the plane to the United States, Coretta still couldn't help but wonder why the Americans had resisted the delegation's efforts to discuss the issue of nuclear testing. The nonviolent protest movement struggled against the inequities of racism, but Coretta also saw sexism as an undeniable and stifling injustice.

In Atlanta, Martin was working hard to strengthen the SCLC's leadership of the nonviolent movement. He also wanted to launch the voter registration campaign, which had taken a backseat to his troubles with the southern legal system. Throughout most of the preceding year, the SCLC had managed to raise as much as $20,000 through a celebrity benefit concert at Carnegie Hall, organized in part by Maya Angelou. Writers, artists, actors, and musicians—both black and white—such as Angelou, Leonard Bernstein, and Harry Belafonte shared their talents to raise money for the nonviolent movement. Some celebrities even made personal donations to the SCLC and the SNCC.

These funds allowed the SCLC to hire new staff members to help Martin with the movement. Ralph Abernathy and his family also moved from Montgomery to Atlanta in order to be closer to the SCLC's headquarters. Wyatt T. Walker, a black minister from Virginia who fought to integrate public facilities in cities throughout that state, was hired to be the SCLC's executive director and run the main headquarters. Andrew Young, another black minister, came to work for the SCLC after collaborating with Martin to increase black voter registration in the South.

Septima Clark and Dorothy Cotton also joined the ranks. Clark headed the SCLC's Citizenship Education Program, which schooled southern

Both Martin and Coretta were baffled by the Kennedy administration's lack of support for desegregating the racist stronghold of Albany, Georgia. Albany police chief Laurie Pritchett is shown here placing Martin under arrest for leading a demonstration.

blacks in their constitutional rights, voting procedures, and basic literacy. Clark was also responsible for training the young adults who worked as teachers in the program. Cotton was responsible for recruiting college students and young activists to participate.

By this time, Ella Baker was devoting most of her energies to the SNCC. She would eventually leave the SCLC to fight racial discrimination on her own; this was partly because Baker found it difficult to assert her leadership in an organization headed by men. Although the SCLC fought against racism, historians note that Baker felt she encountered chauvinism within the organization.

Baker greatly admired Coretta for her dedication to the civil rights struggle. Before she left the SCLC, she gave Coretta these words of advice: "You need to be among the councils of men. You have a lot to say."

Baker's enthusiasm was a perfect match for the SNCC, the SCLC's student division. The young black members were the engine behind the SCLC's voter-registration campaign that began in Albany, Georgia, in the summer of 1961 under the leadership of Charles Sherwood, SNCC's field secretary, and a young man named Cordell Reagan. In the blink of an eye, the voter-registration campaign blossomed into a sit-in protest against segregation in Albany.

Unfortunately, the mass sit-in failed. That winter, Martin and Abernathy traveled to Albany to help the young people negotiate with city officials and police. The two leaders were jailed repeatedly, but were always released before their plight could arouse public sympathy. Black leaders in community-based civil rights groups were deadlocked in their attempts to reach an agreement with the city. Martin tried several times to contact President Kennedy to see whether the federal government would intervene in the negotiations with city officials, but the White House never responded.

After spending a year working in Albany, Martin returned to Atlanta. The young members of the SNCC were bitter and disappointed. Martin, too, was frustrated that he could not break the city's resistance to racial integration, and the Kennedy administration's silence during the yearlong crisis was also unsettling. Meanwhile, Laurie Pritchett, Albany's chief of police, smugly claimed victory. "Albany is as segregated as ever!" Pritchett boasted.

The nonviolent movement was seven years old. Martin now realized that racism, embedded as it was in the hearts and minds of many Americans, would be far more difficult to overcome than even he had imagined. Just as Coretta and her women colleagues were not taken seriously by the U.S. government in Geneva, it seemed that Martin, the SCLC, SNCC, and the entire nonviolent civil rights movement were being dismissed by southern authorities and the federal government.

But Martin and Coretta would not give up. They continued the struggle and grew wiser in the process.

A meeting with President John F. Kennedy and Attorney General Robert Kennedy was at the top of the SCLC's agenda for 1963. In January, Martin, Abernathy, and Fred Shuttlesworth met with the Kennedys to discuss the need for a new civil-rights bill. The Civil Rights Act of 1957 had not proved as effective as the SCLC had hoped; blacks throughout the South continued to suffer. President Kennedy listened but made no promises.

The SCLC went forward with a plan to desegregate a city that was known as a bedrock of white supremacy—Birmingham, Alabama. The city's entrenched hatred of blacks was legendary; hostilities in Montgomery paled by comparison. Throughout the late 1950s and early 1960s, Birmingham witnessed more than 50 cross burnings, along with more than 15 racially motivated bombings. Eugene "Bull" Connor, the city's commissioner of public safety, was known as an ardent racist who used the police to terrorize blacks. Even Alabama governor George Wallace proclaimed proudly that he would do everything in his power to keep the races separate and unequal, so blacks in Birmingham could not appeal to the state government for help.

If Martin and his followers could challenge the racist city and state government authorities and reveal Birmingham's sins to the nation, the nonviolent movement might gain sorely needed momentum.

The SCLC began organizing in Birmingham early in the year.

Coretta was expecting the Kings' fourth child and was approaching her due date. Martin was busy traveling, but he made it back to Atlanta in time to take Coretta to the hospital. On March 28, 1963, Bernice Albertine, the Kings' second daughter and last child, was born. Martin was off to Birmingham the next day.

On April 3, Martin issued a challenge to the city. He declared the start of a mass protest movement to desegregate all of the city's public facilities and transportation systems and to urge local retail stores to hire black employees. Martin spoke at black churches around Birmingham, encouraging people to join the sit-ins and marches. African Americans, both young and old, heeded the call. People who were willing to protest were trained in nonviolent methods of protecting themselves from police brutality. They were also assured that the SCLC would help pay their bail if they were arrested so they could return to the streets to demonstrate. Protests took place at lunch counters and in front of department stores. During the first few days of the protests, more than 300 people were arrested.

The city eventually got an injunction from the state court forbidding protest demonstrations. The court also ruled that only cash could be accepted as payment for bail. This was a big problem for the protesters because the SCLC's cash reserves were running low.

Martin and other SCLC leaders knew they couldn't back down now. They decided to violate the injunction with a march to city hall on Good Friday, April 12, 1963. Martin and Abernathy vowed to demonstrate together and risk being arrested and missing their Easter sermons. Just as they had anticipated, each was arrested and held in solitary confinement in the Birmingham jail.

Coretta and the children waited in Atlanta for word from Martin, but it didn't come. Martin was jailed so often that phone calls from prison had become routine. This time, however, Coretta knew something was wrong. Wyatt T. Walker tried to call Martin at the jail, but he couldn't get through. Lawyers were also barred from seeing Martin or Abernathy. Neither man was allowed to communi-

cate with anyone.

By Easter Sunday, Coretta was so concerned for their welfare that she called the White House. The president was not available, but Attorney General Robert Kennedy returned Coretta's call. She told him that the family had not heard from Martin in three days and asked if the president could find out about her husband's condition.

The attorney general promised to inquire about Martin. Robert Kennedy was well aware of Bull Connor's reputation for racism. He knew that finding out about Martin and Abernathy was not going to be easy.

On Monday, President Kennedy called Coretta to reassure her. He told her that he had spoken to city and police officials in Birmingham. "Your husband will be calling you shortly," the President said confidently.

To Coretta's great relief, Martin called home 15

The Reverend A. D. King uses the top of a car as an impromptu pulpit in an effort to preserve calm in Birmingham during the early-morning hours of May 12, 1963. Coretta later noted that her brother-in-law's home was bombed just one day after Martin, confident that the city would integrate its public facilities, had left Birmingham.

minutes later. He was weary, but unharmed. Coretta told him of her conversation with the president. "So that's why everybody is suddenly being so polite," Martin said wryly.

But he also intimated that Coretta should instruct other SCLC leaders to leak the story of Kennedy's involvement to the press. She contacted Wyatt T. Walker, and media were alerted shortly thereafter.

Martin and Abernathy would spend eight days in prison, but after the SCLC spread the word that President Kennedy had called Coretta, the nation paid attention to Birmingham and to the nonviolent movement.

As soon as Martin and Abernathy were released on April 20, they met with other SCLC leaders at the organization's Birmingham headquarters. The leaders expressed concern that the protest had come to a halt while Martin and Abernathy were in jail. To sustain public interest, the SCLC decided to recruit schoolchildren for the protest. Martin had reservations about enlisting children in the movement, but he also knew that their youth and innocence would drum up popular support for the battle against Birmingham's racists.

On May 2, more than 1,000 children and teenagers marched from Birmingham's Sixteenth Street Baptist Church into town. Bull Connor made over 900 arrests. The next day, more youths joined the march. This time, Connor ordered his men to blast the children with high-pressure fire hoses and to unleash their dogs. Children were soaked with water, bleeding from dog bites, and battered by police clubs. A scuffle broke out between outraged black onlookers and the police.

When he saw the violence on television and in the newspapers, President Kennedy quickly dispatched a negotiator named Burke Marshall to Birmingham to mediate between the SCLC and

Although she avidly recorded scores of Martin's speeches, Coretta knew instantly that the one he made at the March on Washington on August 28, 1963, had the ring of immortality. He greets the crowd at the Lincoln Memorial that day during his now-legendary "I Have a Dream" speech.

white business and civic leaders. By May 10, an agreement had been reached. The city promised to desegregate public places such as stores and parks. Retailers also agreed to integrate their lunch counters and to hire black employees. Furthermore, black and white leaders were to meet regularly to continue resolving their differences.

Tired and relieved, Martin flew home to be with his wife and children. The violence against the children of Birmingham had deeply shaken him and Coretta.

"Of course, that was not the end of it," she later

wrote of the violence in Birmingham. And some of the fresh chaos touched the King family personally. On May 11, Martin's brother, A. D. King, called Atlanta to report that his home in Birmingham had been firebombed. A. D. had helped the SCLC organize several protests in the city. He and his wife and family were not harmed, and he had tried to stem a tide of angry rioters as he stood in the rubble of his house. The Birmingham office where Martin had just stayed was also bombed. The rioting that broke out after the bombings was an expression of black outrage. People were fed up with the cowardly, racist, terrorist tactics of Birmingham's white hate groups.

Martin flew back to the city to help quell the chaos. Meanwhile, President Kennedy made a national television speech and denounced the violence. He also sent federal troops to the city to restore order.

Despite the destruction and turmoil following the negotiations in Birmingham, the SCLC could still claim a real victory against the evil of racial segregation. Events in Birmingham forced the federal government, which had been urging black activists to be patient, to reexamine its position on the matter.

On June 11, 1963, President Kennedy held a press conference and announced his intention to support a civil-rights bill outlawing racial segregation in all public facilities. The bill would give the government the right to sue businesses and organizations that refused to integrate. The civil-rights bill would reinforce the Supreme Court's decision in *Brown v. Board of Education* and pressure states to fully integrate public education systems.

In the wake of the Birmingham events, communities across the South slowly began to organize marches and sit-ins for freedom and justice. The nonviolent movement for civil rights was in full swing. Dr. Martin Luther King Jr. had succeeded in reaching America's heart and conscience.

On August 28, 1963, the spark that ignited in Birmingham shone brightly in the nation's capital. Nearly 250,000 people—black, white, Native American, Latino, Asian, young, old, rich, and poor—marched from the Washington Monument to the steps of the Lincoln Memorial. The March on Washington for Jobs and Freedom was a mass call for justice for all American people, regardless of race, sex, creed, or economic status. It was the largest peaceful mass demonstration in the history of the United States—and Martin was to speak.

Dripping with sweat from the intense heat, the marchers listened as Martin's words filled the air. He proudly stood before a sea of faces and proclaimed his vision for a better day and a great nation. Coretta sat behind her husband on the speaker's platform. Sensing that he had abandoned his prepared speech and that his words were inspired by God, she beamed with pride.

Several years earlier, Coretta had begun recording her husband's church sermons and speeches. She also clipped newspaper articles about his activities and kept a collection of his personal writings about his evolving philosophy of peace and social justice. Somehow Coretta knew that this speech—articulating Martin's most cherished vision and dream—would be the most meaningful of his life. His words were simple and profound:

> I have a dream that my four little children one day will live in a nation where they will not be judged by the color of their skin, but by the content of their character. I have a dream today!

As Martin left the platform, applause and cheers filled the air. Martin and Coretta left the stage arm in arm as security guards rushed to protect them from the crush of the crowd.

8
"WHAT ARE YOU AFRAID OF?"

"Tragedy came snapping on the heels of triumph," wrote Coretta in *My Life with Martin Luther King, Jr.*, describing what occurred in Birmingham on September 15, 1963. Just weeks after Martin's triumphant speech in Washington, D. C., the Sixteenth Street Baptist Church in Atlanta was bombed. Four young girls were killed. That June, Medgar Evers, head of the NAACP in Mississippi and a friend of Martin's, had been shot to death in his own doorway. Even as she and Martin enjoyed hard-won triumphs, incidents such as these were horrifying reminders to Coretta of how much work was still to be done.

She was at home with Martin and the children in Atlanta when an event that shattered the calm of the entire nation was reported on television. President John F. Kennedy was shot during a trip to Dallas, Texas. It was November 22, 1963.

Coretta was talking to a friend on the telephone. Martin was upstairs watching television. His heart sank as he listened to the report from Dallas.

When not working for civil rights, Coretta took a stand against nuclear-weapons testing. She is shown here at a Women Strike for Peace rally on the United Nations Plaza in November 1963. She had accompanied the group to a conference in Switzerland the previous year.

Celebrating in song: Coretta and the King children (left to right: Yolanda, Bernice, Dexter, and Martin III) gather around the piano after Martin was named the winner of the 1964 Nobel Peace Prize. King himself was in an Atlanta hospital for a checkup when the news broke.

"Corrie," Martin yelled, "I just heard that President Kennedy has been shot—maybe killed!"

Coretta hung up the phone and rushed upstairs. The Kings watched the news in silence. The update they were dreading finally came: the president was dead.

Martin and Coretta looked at each other in disbelief. The loss of President Kennedy was a devastating blow both personally and politically. The president had been an ally in the nonviolent movement and a supporter of the SCLC's goals in troubled times. "This is what is going to happen to me also," Martin finally said in a flat voice. "I keep telling you, this is a sick society."

Coretta stared at her husband. There was nothing she could say. She simply held her husband's hand. "I felt he was right," she admitted later.

Martin became depressed for a time after the assassination, leaving Atlanta only to attend the president's funeral in Washington, D.C. Kennedy had been killed just as he was trying to pass civil-rights legislation through Congress. But on July 2, 1964, President Lyndon B. Johnson, the former vice president, signed Kennedy's civil-rights bill into law. Martin was one of several black civic and religious leaders invited to the White House to witness the event. The president gave Martin one of the pens he had used to sign the document. King's first meeting with Johnson helped reassure him that the new president was on the side of civil rights.

The SCLC pushed forward with a voter registration campaign in Selma, Alabama—a city 30 miles from Coretta's hometown—where 15,000 blacks were eligible to vote, but only 383 were registered. The SNCC had tried to mount a grassroots campaign there the previous year, but the Selma police had clamped down on the voter education classes they held in local schools and churches.

Throughout the summer and early fall of 1964, Martin continued to travel—to Germany and to the Vatican for a private audience with Pope Paul VI— and to help the SCLC and SNCC with their voter registration drive. Coretta was busy giving Freedom Concerts.

But she was not too busy to worry about Martin's health, and she convinced him to go to an Atlanta hospital for a complete checkup in October.

Soon after Martin was admitted, Coretta received a call from a reporter who had exciting news: the Reverend Dr. Martin Luther King Jr. had won the Nobel Peace Prize for 1964. The award is

The whirl of ceremonies that surrounded the awarding of the Nobel Peace Prize gave Martin and Coretta a relatively rare chance to simply enjoy themselves as a couple. Here, Martin gets a kiss from his wife during a celebratory dinner in Atlanta.

one of the most prestigious honors in the world, funded by the estate of the late Swedish inventor Alfred Bernhard Nobel and by grants from the Central Bank of Sweden. Nobel Peace Prize winners are selected by a Norwegian committee on the basis of their outstanding efforts to bring peace to humankind. At only 35, Martin was the youngest person ever to have received the award. In addition to the honor of being selected, Martin won a cash prize of $54,000.

Coretta immediately called Martin at the hospital. "How is the Nobel Peace Prize winner for 1964 feeling this morning?" she asked her drowsy husband—who thought he was still dreaming.

Once he had realized that Coretta's news was no

dream, Martin set up a press conference at the hospital. The SCLC office called Coretta and gave her the details. She was at his side in the hospital as Martin humbly thanked the Nobel Committee for giving him the world's greatest humanitarian award. He pledged to spend the entire cash prize on advancing civil rights. A few days later, Martin left the hospital with a clean bill of health.

The King family joyously made preparations for the trip to Norway for the award ceremony. A group of local ministers paid for plane tickets for Martin's parents. Although the children were anxious to go, no one under age 12 was allowed at the ceremony.

Before flying to Norway, Coretta flew to New York on November 14 to begin another series of national Freedom Concerts to raise money for the SCLC. She performed an eight-part composition called "The Story of the Struggle from 1955 to 1965" at New York City's Town Hall. Her rendition of the story set to music raised $6,000 for the movement. In early December, she performed a second concert in New Jersey.

She then returned to Atlanta to accompany her husband and a group of 30 family members and friends to Norway to see Martin receive the Nobel Peace Prize. During a stop in London, Martin preached a sermon at St. Paul's Cathedral. On December 8, the Kings arrived in Oslo, Norway, and were greeted by officials from the Nobel Committee. Two days later, in a ceremony at Oslo University, King Olav V of Norway presented Dr. Martin Luther King Jr. with the Nobel Peace Prize: a gold medal, a scroll, and a cash prize. After the ceremony, family and friends gathered at the King's hotel suite to toast Martin with champagne. It was an emotional high point of Martin and Coretta's life together.

Meanwhile, voter-registration campaigns in Selma, Alabama, and nearby Marion were becoming dangerous and bloody. One protest march led to the death of a young black man whose aunt was a childhood friend of Coretta's. On February 26, 1965, Jimmie Lee Jackson died of a gunshot wound he had sustained eight days earlier when he was trying to protect his mother from an attack by a state trooper.

On February 1, shortly before Jackson's death, Martin and Abernathy were jailed in Selma. They spent five days in prison because they refused to pay bail. Every attempt the SCLC made to register black voters was thwarted. Selma's mayor, the chief of police, and Governor George Wallace did all they could to break down the campaign.

Coretta and Juanita Abernathy went to Selma during their husbands' imprisonment. Soon after their arrival, Coretta learned that former Black Muslim leader Malcolm X was in the local African Methodist Episcopal church, and that he had roused the beleaguered demonstrators with his message, which condoned retaliatory violence. Coretta entered the church and took a turn addressing the crowd, stressing the importance of nonviolence. When she met Malcolm, Coretta found him apologetic about any difficulty his presence had caused that day. He also expressed regret at not being able to visit Martin in jail. The assassination of Malcolm X on February 21, 1965, a short time after their meeting, left Coretta both saddened and ambivalent towards some of the slain leader's beliefs, which had been more separatist than those of Martin and the SCLC.

On March 5, Martin flew to Washington, D.C., and informed President Johnson that the campaign would not succeed without a federal voting rights bill to eliminate discriminatory laws. The president assured Martin that he would draft such a bill.

The next day, police, under the command of Selma's sheriff, Jim Clark, attacked more than 150

black students who were demonstrating peacefully outside a city courthouse. Clark's men forced the students to jog towards a jail six miles outside of town, shocking them repeatedly with electric cattle prods to keep them going at a fast clip. Sickened by the events in Selma, Martin announced that the SCLC would sponsor a march from Selma to Montgomery—a distance of over 50 miles—to force Governor Wallace to rein in police and to demand justice at the ballot box.

The first march, which Martin organized but did not lead, took place on Sunday, March 7, 1965. But as over 500 marchers reached the Edmund Pettus bridge on their way to Montgomery, they were greeted by a barricade of hostile Alabama state troopers and mounted calvarymen who ordered them to turn back. When they refused, they were chased back. In addition to cattle prods, the

Coretta walks with Martin on March 25, 1965, the final day of the SCLC's successful march from Selma to Montgomery, Alabama. Coretta could not join her husband on the march until its second day because of a speaking engagement.

protesters now faced brutal beatings, lashings with bullwhips, and being trampled under the horses and choked with tear gas.

Coretta got word of this "Bloody Sunday" just before giving a Freedom Concert in San Francisco as part of a six-city West Coast tour. When Martin called her later, he was upset that his followers had suffered so much in his absence. He planned to personally lead another march that Tuesday, with Ralph Abernathy at his side. But Alabama officials had gotten a federal injunction against the scheduled march. Coretta supported Martin's plans to march, although she knew he faced grave danger. She also called the children in Atlanta to assure them that their father was all right.

On March 9, roughly half of the 1,500 marchers who followed King from Selma were white. But one striking similarity between this march and the tragic attempt made two days earlier remained: they were again met by a blockade of troopers and horsemen at the Edmund Pettus Bridge. After a tense silence, King ordered the marchers to turn back. Although he faced much criticism for his decision, it probably averted needless bloodshed.

President Johnson had been watching the developments in Selma. The injunction against marching from Selma to Montgomery was lifted, and Johnson overrode Governor Wallace, taking control of the Alabama National Guard and assigning them to protect the civil-rights marchers.

On March 21, Martin, the SCLC leadership, and thousands of supporters left Selma for Montgomery on a four-day march. Coretta, who had a speaking engagement at Bennett College in North Carolina that day, joined Martin on the second day of the march. The marchers sang gospel songs and chanted "We want freedom!" for miles, on a trek that was punctuated by rain and mud. When they reached Montgomery, the marchers passed Dexter

Avenue Baptist Church—the site of Martin's first pastorate—and came to the steps of the state capitol.

On August 6, 1965, President Johnson signed the Voting Rights Act. Coupled with the Civil Rights Act of 1964, the Voting Rights Act signaled the demise of the southern system of racial discrimination that had existed since slavery.

That fall, Coretta enrolled Yoki and Marty in one of the best all-white public schools in Atlanta. The King children did not want to be the only two black children in school, so Coretta convinced Juanita Abernathy to register her three children in the Spring Street School as well. The school's principal made them feel welcome, but made it clear that she did not want reporters lurking around her school. But outside the school, Coretta was very open with the media about the King family's decision to help integrate Atlanta's school system. This was one time when Coretta wanted the entire nation to see her children walking in their father's footsteps.

The SCLC's victories in its southern campaigns, impressive as they were, merely scratched the surface of racism in the nation. In larger cities throughout the North, blacks also suffered, living in ghettos that separated them from the mainstream of American life.

Black families often struggled for survival in cramped housing projects neglected by city landlords. Blacks also had little access to adequate health care or social services. The rate of unemployment among northern urban blacks was high compared to other racial groups. Education at predominantly black public schools was usually inferior to that offered by schools in all-white neighborhoods, and school buildings in ghetto areas were frequently decrepit and poorly equipped.

In June 1966, the Kings moved to Chicago to

wage a war against urban poverty. The SCLC led a mass march to the city hall in July. When the marchers reached their destination, Martin nailed a list of demands for Mayor Richard Daley onto the door. It was a symbolic gesture that recalled his namesake Martin Luther's nailing of the Ninety-Five Theses to a door at Germany's University of Wittenburg in 1517. King's list outlined demands for fairness in public housing and for the integration of white neighborhoods. Coretta and all of the children marched with Martin on this historic day.

The next day, however, was less auspicious. Mayor Daley, having reviewed Martin's list of demands, dismissed them all in a meeting that morning.

As news of this decision spread, discouragement hung in the oppressive summer air in the ghetto. Life in a Chicago public housing unit was a jarring adjustment for the King family. Coretta noted with grim amusement that the landlord had haphazardly painted the apartment in anticipation of his famous tenant. But the hallways still reeked of urine, the plumbing and heating were still substandard, and "there was nothing green in sight" as far as playgrounds for children were concerned.

The evening after Martin's meeting with Mayor Daley, he and Coretta were driving to another meeting. They saw a crowd of young people rioting in the street. Police told them that some neighborhood children had turned on the fire hydrants to cool themselves. When police shut off the hydrants, the kids started throwing rocks and breaking windows; then, local gangs got involved, shooting started, and the violence escalated. Coretta, Martin, and SCLC leaders spent that night on the streets of Chicago, trying to find the deeper causes of the rioting and to promote nonviolence. Fortunately, the children were away visiting with friends that night.

Scattered rioting stretched into the next day,

during which Coretta spoke at a women's meeting at the local YWCA. "I was supposed to talk about unity, but that was hardly the day for it," she recalled in her autobiography. The neighborhood women shared her mood. When it was suggested that they send a telegram to Mayor Daley urging him to support the SCLC's list of fair housing demands, many of them were reluctant to sign it. Coretta guessed that perhaps their husbands held city jobs and the women feared that they could be fired.

Giving a concert in Columbus, Ohio, May 1965. Even before the assassination of her husband, Coretta was in demand as a speaker and singer in her own right.

"What are you afraid of?" Coretta finally asked. "There comes a time when we have to make a decision and we have to make a choice." The women responded by not only signing the telegram, but also by forming an integrated organization which came to be known as Women Mobilized for Change, dedicated to improving local living conditions. In time the group's membership grew to over 1,000 women.

The rioting continued the next day. Coretta had to deliver another speech, and this time she took the children with her. They then waited out the chaos in their small apartment without Martin, who was out among the people trying to restore order.

After the rioting ended, two black people, one of them a 14-year-old girl, were dead. The SCLC decided to make integrating Chicago's housing its top priority. Marches into all-white, working-class neighborhoods were scheduled. Mayor Daley, who was up for reelection, worried that he would lose the support of white voters if such marches were held. But Martin moved forward in his fight to make safe, clean housing a reality for his people.

Martin personally led a march into Marquette Park on August 5, 1966. That day, 600 people—including many whites—followed him through Chicago's white communities. The residents' responses were horrifying. People threw rocks and bottles at the marchers. Some shouted insults like "Nigger!", "Coon!", and "Go back to Africa!" Martin later told Coretta that he had never experienced such intense hatred—not even in the deep South. During the march he was hit in the head with a rock.

On August 26, Mayor Daley and heads of several city agencies finally agreed to call a truce with the SCLC. The mayor feared that further marching by the SCLC would alienate his white supporters and incite additional mayhem in the streets. The city agreed to redirect its financial and social resources to improve living conditions in the ghettos and to integrate all-white communities. When Martin and Coretta left Chicago, the city's black residents had hope for better lives.

In 1967, Martin's lifelong dedication to nonviolence and Christian love was challenged when he decided to denounce America's involvement in the Vietnam War. Thousands of miles away, young American soldiers were fighting and dying in a bitter war pitting South Vietnam against North Vietnam and the Communist rebels it supported. The United States had backed the South Vietnamese government since the late 1950s, but its military mission was taking a dreadful toll in human lives and American tax dollars.

Specifically, King noted that the government spent far more money in pursuit of a single Vietcong casualty than it would cost to help a single poor person in this country. Furthermore, a disproportionate number of the young American soldiers dying in Vietnam were poor blacks who could not avoid the draft. "A nation that continues year after year to spend more on military defense than on programs of social uplift is approaching spiritual death," Martin said in a speech before a group of clergymen at Riverside Church in New York City that April.

Coretta agreed with him. She had actively participated in the peace movement for years, and was glad to see Martin beginning to embrace a worldwide push for peace as part of his nonviolent philosophy. But many black civil-rights leaders criticized Martin for shifting his attention away from the black struggle for equality. Also, some blacks agreed with the U.S. government's position on Vietnam, so he risked alienating them from the civil-rights movement.

These criticisms notwithstanding, Martin's call for peace in Vietnam fell on deaf ears. Throughout the summer of 1967, riots broke out in many U.S.

The gutted remains of a city block on Chicago's west side on April 6, 1968, two days after Martin's murder. Less than two years earlier, he and Coretta had walked the streets of Chicago attempting to quell two days of rioting that had stemmed from the frustration felt by the city's poor.

cities. Blacks were dissatisfied with the gradual pace of the nonviolent movement; many whites, on the other hand, felt threatened by the incremental progress of civil-rights laws. Martin himself was frustrated and in search of new ways of bringing people together.

His answer was the Poor People's Campaign— an initiative to organize the nation's poor, regardless of race, from 10 cities and 5 rural towns in a mass protest to demand "economic security, decent sanitary housing, and quality education" for every American. The protesters would build a tent city in the heart of Washington, D.C., to demonstrate their plight. The nonviolent movement was slowly shifting its focus from a civil-rights struggle into a human rights struggle.

In February 1968, the Sanitation Workers Union in Memphis, Tennessee, went on strike to protest unfair treatment by the mayor. The predominantly black union had tried for several weeks to launch a mass march, but the city's police were blocking their every move. A union leader and SCLC contact in Memphis called Martin and asked him to help the garbage collectors mount a protest. He agreed to help.

But the event was a disaster. Martin arrived in Memphis to discover the march already in progress—and terribly undisciplined, with no lines formed and some of the marchers advocating violence.

It was violence that brought the protest to an abrupt halt. One man was shot during the frenzy. Martin returned to Atlanta to recover from the turmoil. He was deeply troubled. It was the first time extreme disorder had occurred during a march under his leadership. He wanted to go back to Memphis as soon as possible to prove that nonviolent tactics could work.

Other SCLC leaders disagreed. They felt that Martin should direct his energies toward the Poor People's Campaign. Martin's associates also worried about his safety. The discussion over his next project turned into a heated debate. SCLC staff members were eager to move on. Martin, however, was determined to make things right in Memphis.

Not only was he troubled by the prospect of a lost battle in Memphis; he was now deeply saddened by the division among his own staff. "Martin is extremely depressed," a colleague of his told Coretta during a phone call. She was in Washington, D.C., attending a press conference for the Women's International League for Peace and Freedom. She had heard about the trouble in Memphis and called to check on Martin.

But back in Atlanta, Martin soon pulled himself together, and the SCLC made plans to return to Memphis.

On Wednesday, April 3, Coretta awoke before dawn to cook breakfast for Martin and Abernathy before their trip to the airport. The two men were tense. They knew that going back to Memphis was a risky endeavor. Abernathy kept looking at his watch; Martin fumbled around the house, trying to get dressed in time to catch their seven o'clock flight. Neither man ate any of the breakfast Coretta had prepared.

When Coretta later recalled kissing her husband good-bye, she described it as a farewell "like thousands of other times before." The two men dashed to Abernathy's car, and Coretta watched them drive down the street as the sun peeked over the horizon. She would never see Martin alive again.

In Memphis that evening, he stood before a crowd of 2,000 supporters outside a church. Martin told the crowd that he would lead a second march on April 8, despite a federal injunction that the city had secured to stop the protest. He said the march was more than a demonstration for local garbage collectors; it was a public testament to the moral justice of nonviolence and proof that no evil could match the Christian belief in the power of love.

He told the crowd that his flight was delayed that morning for a bomb search. He shared with them his knowledge of threats against his life. But Martin assured them that none of this would make him retreat to Atlanta.

"Then," as Coretta wrote in My Life with Martin Luther King, Jr., "the mantle of prophecy seemed to descend upon Martin."

"Like anybody else, I would like to live a long life," he said in his speech against the eerie backdrop of a spring storm that was brewing outside.

"Longevity has its place. But I'm not concerned with that now. I just want to do God's will."

Friends and associates told Coretta that Martin's sense of humor had returned on April 4 after his somber speech of the previous night. He was light-hearted and joked around with his brother A. D., Abernathy, Andrew Young, and other SCLC members in his room at the Lorraine Motel. Martin and A. D. even called their mother in Atlanta to share a few laughs.

Later that evening, Martin, Abernathy, and a local minister named Samuel B. Kyles decided to go out to dinner before attending a civil-rights meeting. When Kyles headed down to the hotel parking lot and Abernathy went back into the room, Martin stood alone on the balcony.

He was fatally shot in that instant.

9

BLACK MADONNA

The Rev. Dr. Martin Luther King Jr.'s death marked the end of an era in the history of civil rights. Even in those first bleak days after her husband's death, Coretta knew that his dream must not be allowed to die with him.

There were countless newspaper stories covering her husband's funeral. Reporters compared Coretta's demeanor with the dignified air of former first lady Jacqueline Kennedy at President Kennedy's funeral in 1963. Words such as grace, resilience, courage, and strength were frequently used in reports about Coretta. One reporter, after observing her during the funeral service at Ebenezer Baptist Church, described Coretta as the "Black Madonna"—an African-American counterpart to Mary, the mother of Jesus, during the crucifixion of her only son.

This flood of praise may have come as a surprise to Coretta, who later wrote admiringly of Mrs. Kennedy's deportment during the president's funeral. Despite her quiet courage, Coretta felt vulnerable even as she consoled her children and attended to Martin's unfinished business affairs. Coretta's religious faith and the love and concern of friends from near and far were her only anchors.

Harry Belafonte provided a shoulder for Coretta to lean on. Martin had not made elaborate plans for

Coretta's strength and dignity under wrenching circumstances won the respect and admiration of people around the world.

his family's financial security in the event of his death. Coretta knew that her husband was not concerned about wealth or possessions. He gave most of his earnings to the nonviolent movement and reportedly set aside just $5,000 for his family. According to *Ebony* magazine, Belafonte had taken out a $500,000 insurance policy in Martin's name years before Martin's death. The policy helped to assure Coretta that her children would be taken care of.

During the next few weeks, Coretta kept in close contact with the SCLC. Much of Martin's immediate work had to be completed; Coretta knew this was not the time to become consumed by grief. She honored as many of her husband's public appearances and speaking engagements as possible. An antiwar rally in Central Park was planned for April 27, which happened to be Coretta's birthday, and the Poor People's Campaign could not be canceled. She knew she had to attend both events because they were perfect opportunities to continue Martin's plans to promote justice and peace. She searched through Martin's personal papers and found notes for a speech he was preparing for the antiwar rally called "The 10 Commandments on Vietnam." Coretta relied on Martin's notes to make her presentation.

On May 2, 1968, Coretta helped to launch the Poor People's Campaign from the balcony of the Lorraine Motel in Memphis. Martin's brother stood with her as she unveiled a plaque to honor her late husband. She knew this was the place where Martin was struck down in the prime of life, but Coretta stood tall. She looked out at the audience of 1,000 people and spoke earnestly.

"I pledge eternal loyalty to the work my husband nobly began," she said. "His legacy will lead us to the point where all God's children have shoes."

The crowd followed Coretta as she marched

through the streets of Memphis. She walked behind a mule-drawn wagon, reminiscent of the one that had carried Martin to his gravesite in Atlanta. The marchers later traveled by bus to Mississippi to join others who were bound for the nation's capital.

Several weeks later, Coretta walked arm in arm with Abernathy, now president of the SCLC, during the largest rally of the Campaign, the Solidarity Day march on June 19. Fifty thousand citizens—a rainbow of faces—came to show their support of Martin's dream of an integrated society. Coretta, wearing a black dress, low-heeled black shoes, and sunglasses, wore a white lily over her heart. She delivered the speech for her husband's last scheduled public appearance on the steps of the Lincoln Memorial.

"The problem[s] of racism, poverty, and war can all be summarized with one word—violence," Coretta declared. Yoki, Martin III, Dexter, and little Bernice watched their mother from the stage platform, surrounded by SCLC members and family. As Coretta spoke, her years as a peace activist showed. She spoke not only as the widow of Dr. Martin Luther King Jr., but also as a woman and a mother. "Women, if the soul of this nation is to be saved, I believe that you must become its soul. You must speak out against the evils of our time as you see them," Coretta said. She urged women of all races to build a "solid block of women's power" for peace and equality in the world.

Her speech broke new ground. Few women, regardless of race, had ever had the opportunity to address the social, political, and economic ills of the nation in front of such a large gathering. Not only was she able to further her late husband's agenda for social change, but she also sent a rallying cry to American women by entreating them to join the front lines of the nonviolent struggle for human rights. Once again, Coretta's determination

On the balcony of the Lorraine Motel outside the room Martin occupied before his murder, Coretta launches the Poor People's Campaign, May 2, 1968. Ralph Abernathy stands to her right.

impressed reporters. The *New York Times* called her "a woman champion of equality for all races."

But winning personal adulation wasn't Coretta's goal. In July, she held a press conference in Atlanta to announce her plans to build the Martin Luther King Jr. Center for Nonviolent Social Change. The King Center would be located along two blocks of Auburn Avenue and would include the restoration of her husband's birthplace in addition to his gravesite, a library and archive of his personal writings, a memorial park, a museum, and an institute dedicated to nonviolent social change and African-American studies. Coretta also told the nation about her fund-raising campaign to cover the costs of building the King Center. To collect donations for the project, Coretta vowed to travel throughout the United States and the world, spreading Dr. Martin Luther King's message of love and hope to people everywhere.

Coretta also signed a contract with a major New York publisher, worth $50,000 according to press reports, to write the story of her life with Martin throughout the struggle for civil rights. She spent the rest of the summer alone in New England writing the book.

Later, Coretta filed legal papers to make the King Center a nonprofit corporation and selected a board of directors to administer its affairs. She became the center's chief executive officer.

On January 15, 1969, Coretta celebrated Martin's 40th birthday in a ceremony at Ebenezer Baptist Church. Two days later, she formally announced the establishment of the King Center as a nonprofit organization before leaving on a tour of Italy and India.

Coretta visited Rome and met Pope Paul at the Vatican. She also received the Italian government's Universal Love Award, becoming the first non-Italian so honored. In India, Coretta accepted the Nehru Award on behalf of her husband. Before leaving this place that Martin loved, Coretta gave a series of speeches.

In the spring of 1969, Coretta and her sister Edythe traveled to London. Coretta became the first woman to give a sermon at St. Paul's Cathedral—the same church Martin had visited in 1964 before accepting the Nobel Peace Prize. She also performed several Freedom Concerts throughout Britain, Germany, and Holland.

Coretta returned home in May. Abernathy invited her to help lead a strike of black hospital workers organized by Local 1199-B of the Drug and Hospital Union in Charleston, South Carolina. The majority of the strikers were women who worked as nurse's aides, licensed practical nurses, housekeepers, and laundry workers. Abernathy and the local chapter of the SCLC believed Coretta's presence would inspire the picketers.

Coretta left Atlanta for Charleston, just as her husband had left for Memphis to help the striking garbage collectors only a year before. When she arrived, Abernathy and several hundred black strikers were already in prison. Coretta gave a speech before 7,000 union supporters at a local church. She also led a two-mile march to Charleston Hospital. National Guardsmen were called to keep the protesters in check, but Coretta was not afraid.

Coretta later served as an honorary chairperson of a committee for the Drug and Hospital Union. She worked with union leaders to make sure the workers' rights were protected.

In September, Coretta's first book, *My Life with Martin Luther King, Jr.*, was published. Her memories could now be shared with millions of readers in America and around the world. But Coretta's autobiography was not the only literary high point of her year. The American Library Association honored her by establishing the Coretta Scott King Award for outstanding black writers and illustrators of children's literature. The award has been given every year since 1969 to writers and artists whose work exemplifies Dr. King's dream of equality and Coretta's dedication to world peace.

Coretta's involvement with the arts had always gone beyond having awards named in her honor, though. In 1971, she followed up her master's degree in music from the New England Conservatory with a doctorate.

She also continued to travel, delivering speeches, participating in protests, receiving numerous awards and honors, and networking with powerful people.

After Martin's death, Coretta was elected to the SCLC's board of directors. But the alliance between King's widow and the male-dominated SCLC was not an easy one, according to some reports. "Much

Coretta revisited St. Paul's Cathedral in London—where Martin had spoken in 1964—making some history of her own in the process. Her sermon, which took place on March 6, 1969, was the first ever given at St. Paul's by a woman.

of our male leadership that honored Dr. King, worshipped Dr. King, find it hard to recognize the strength in a woman like Coretta King," said Dorothy Height, president of the National Council of Negro Women, in an interview with the *Washington Post* 20 years after Martin's death. "It is easier for them to think of her as the widow of a martyr than giving leadership in her own right."

Coretta had always been outspoken in her own right, but Martin's death had given her a permanent place in the national spotlight. Remembering Ella Baker's words of wisdom, she knew it was her responsibility to speak her mind and move forward with her own vision. To that end, Coretta began to work independently of the SCLC.

Black members of Congress began lobbying their colleagues to support a federal holiday in honor of Martin. Representative John Conyers (D-MI) was one of the first congressmen to introduce such a bill, just four days after Martin's assassination. The idea met with little support, however.

Coretta joined a coalition of politicians, civil-rights advocates, and peace activists in a national effort to make Martin's birthday a national holiday. In 1971, the *Washington Post* reported that King supporters led a mule-drawn wagon to Washington, D.C., and dropped three million petitions supporting the holiday on the steps of the Capitol building. Congress paid little attention to the demonstration, but Coretta continued to travel across the country, calling for a "truly American holiday" that people of every race could celebrate.

Coretta's influence as a civil-rights activist grew steadily during the 1970s. Candidates for national and state office began to seek her endorsement for their campaigns. Governor George McGovern sought her support in his campaign for president, as did black congressional candidate Ron Dellums.

President Jimmy Carter, a great admirer of Coretta's, appointed her as a public delegate to the United Nations. Coretta later cochaired a committee to support the Humphrey-Hawkins Full Employment and Balanced Growth Act, a federal law stating that every American citizen had the right to a job at decent pay and under safe working conditions. Congress later approved the legislation. To combat sexism, Coretta went to Congress to lobby for the passage of the Equal Rights Amendment (E.R.A.) for women.

In 1979, Representative John Conyers once again introduced the King holiday bill on the floor of Congress, but the measure fell just five votes short of passage. This time, Coretta was more determined than ever to get the legislation passed. Several states had already passed their own King holiday bills, but Coretta knew the holiday would have little meaning unless it was observed by the entire nation.

President Carter agreed to approve the legislation if it passed his desk before the end of his term. But Coretta and her allies faced staunch political opponents—most notably Senators Strom Thurmond (R-SC) and Jesse Helms (R-NC)—both of whom questioned whether Martin's achievements merited a national holiday.

Coretta went to the nation's capital and had a personal meeting with Representative Jack Kemp (R-NY) to persuade him to back the King bill. "It [was] a powerful thing to meet Mrs. Martin Luther King, Jr.," Kemp told the *Washington Post* in 1986. "I just felt like it [supporting the King holiday legislation] was the right thing to do." After the meeting, Kemp lobbied his colleagues to support the bill.

The King holiday campaign was one of the most popular public endeavors in recent history. In 1980, Grammy Award–winning singer and musician Stevie Wonder wrote a song called "Happy Birthday" that became the anthem for the crusade. In that same year, the U.S. National Park Service declared Dr. King's childhood home and the surrounding neighborhood on Auburn Avenue a historic district in order to preserve the area. Encouraged, Coretta and the King Center staff started another petition drive to support the King holiday. Coretta was not going to give up.

Coretta stood in her husband's place for a very

When Coretta coordinated a 20th anniversary celebration of the March on Washington, longtime friend Harry Belafonte was on hand to give a concert at the Lincoln Memorial. The celebration reaffirmed the message of Martin's often-quoted "I Have a Dream" speech.

special memorial on August 28, 1983. To commemorate the 20th anniversary of the March on Washington, the King Center sponsored a New Coalition of Conscience to advocate a 12-point plan to promote jobs, peace, and freedom. A proposal for the King holiday was part of the plan. Standing on the steps of the Lincoln Memorial, Coretta and the leaders of other civil-rights and peace groups reiterated Martin's call for social justice. This time, 500,000 people publicly showed their support for a national holiday in honor of Dr. King. As Martin's birthday anthem filled the air, Coretta clapped and sang along, hoping that President Ronald Reagan and Congress were listening.

Three months later, on November 2, Coretta went to the White House to watch President Reagan sign legislation that established the third Monday in January as the official celebration of the birthday of Rev. Dr. Martin Luther King Jr.

Senator Helms, however, opposed the King holiday. He alleged that Dr. King had affiliations with the Communist Party USA during the civil-rights movement and questioned King's allegiance to the U.S. government. To prove his allegations, Helms wanted to examine sealed FBI files on King, but a judge refused his request.

Several weeks before signing the bill, President Reagan, who at first opposed the holiday, commented in a press conference that he did not fault Senator Helms for "wanting the records opened up" to investigate Dr. King's alleged affiliations with the Communist Party. The president's statement caused many black leaders to question his support for civil rights. Later, the president reportedly called Coretta to apologize for his statement at the press conference.

As she witnessed the signing, Coretta Scott King smiled while several other black leaders and civil-rights colleagues sang "We Shall Overcome." She had proven over the years that she had the will, foresight, and know-how to keep her husband's legacy alive.

10

THE DREAM CONTINUES

❧

January 15, 1986, marked the first official national holiday in honor of Dr. Martin Luther King Jr. Coretta and her four children celebrated the historic occasion at the King Center and sponsored a program called "Ending the Violence of Poverty, World Hunger, and Apartheid Through Creative Nonviolent Actions." Coretta also led the first King holiday march though the streets of Atlanta. From this day forward, Americans would remember Dr. King's lifelong commitment to the full equality of all human beings.

"We promote it as a holiday for people of all races, religions and color[s]," Coretta told journalist Barbara Reynolds in 1988. "I would be disappointed if it turned out to be a black holiday. He [King] was all inclusive."

Coretta was named chairperson of the Martin Luther King Jr. Federal Holiday Commission in Washington, D.C., to coordinate celebration activities in communities across the nation.

By the time of the first observance of the King holiday, the King Center was an established institution. The Center now includes an interdenominational chapel, exhibit halls, seminar rooms, a 250-seat auditorium, and an international conference and cultural center capable of translating numerous languages. Workshops on conflict resolu-

On August 27, 1993, Coretta met with Sarah Brady, who helped pen the Brady Bill for handgun control after her husband, James, was paralyzed by an assassin's bullet during the 1981 attempt on President Ronald Reagan's life. The two women joined forces to help get the bill enacted, with Coretta pledging the support of the Martin Luther King Jr. Foundation to Brady's group, Handgun Control Inc.

tion, nonviolent protest techniques, and community development are also held.

The King Center opened its doors to the public in 1982. Since then, more than a million people from around the world have come to visit the historic site each year. Coretta's fund-raising efforts to build the center were extraordinary: over $10 million in contributions were reportedly collected.

Coretta's achievements did not end with the establishment of the King holiday and the King Memorial Center, though. Her next campaign was the battle against the oppressive all-white government of South Africa and its racist policy of apartheid.

Since 1910, the South African government had ruled black Africans with an iron fist. Blacks were not allowed to own land or live in cities. They were segregated in barren, overcrowded areas called "homelands." Blacks also worked at menial, low-paying jobs and had to send their children to dismal schools. They were not even allowed to vote.

Nelson Mandela, a black African lawyer who helped lead a freedom movement in South Africa during the late 1950s and early 1960s, was sent to prison by the government on charges of treason in 1964. He was given a life sentence.

Coretta and scores of other human rights activists in the United States and around the world participated in demonstrations to protest the South African government's policies and Mandela's imprisonment. In 1984, Coretta was invited by the United Nations Special Committee Against Apartheid to be the keynote speaker at its International Day of Solidarity with the Women of South Africa and Namibia. A year later, Coretta, Martin III, and Bernice were arrested during a rally in front of the South African Embassy in Washington, D.C.

Coretta supported trade sanctions against the South African government that were intended to cripple that nation's economy and force its leaders to recognize the black majority. In 1988, the King Center sent a delegation to South Africa on a fact-finding mission to document evidence of racial discrimination and government repression.

Coretta was especially drawn to the South African freedom struggle because Mandela and his wife Winnie appeared to walk the same path she and Martin had traveled during their years together. Coretta knew too well the indignities of government oppression and the personal sacrifices needed to lead a nation toward the goal of social justice and peace. The African-American and South African struggles for human rights were inextricably linked.

International economic and political pressure against apartheid, coupled with decades of bloody violence, finally broke the back of the South African government. In 1990, South African president F. W. de Klerk released Nelson Mandela from prison. Mandela had earned the admiration of the entire world. His people saw him as a symbol of hope in desperate times—just as black Americans had come to regard Martin.

To express their thanks to their American supporters, Nelson and Winnie Mandela came to the United States for a national tour. Coretta welcomed the Mandelas to America and introduced Nelson to excited well-wishers at a rally in Atlanta.

Four years later, on May 2, 1994, Coretta stood on a podium with Mandela in South Africa after his nation's first nonracial government election on April 27. It was the first time the black majority had exercised their newly won right to vote.

Nelson Mandela defeated President de Klerk and became the new leader of South Africa. The South African freedom movement had come full circle. Coretta, a spiritual sister of the new democratic nation, had done her part to help make this day happen.

After Nelson Mandela's 1990 release from prison in South Africa, Coretta welcomed him to America. Here she presents the antiapartheid leader with the first-ever Martin Luther King Jr. International Freedom Award during his visit to Atlanta.

Today, Coretta Scott King can look back proudly on a lifetime of social service and commitment. Her children are healthy and productive adults. Yolanda is an actress and film producer; Martin III is a businessman in Atlanta; and Bernice, who also holds a law degree, is a pastor at the Greater Rising Star Baptist Church, also in Atlanta.

In October 1994, Coretta stepped down as CEO and president of the Martin Luther King Jr. Center for Nonviolent Social Change and handed the reins of leadership to her son Dexter Scott. Dexter works with a 36-member board of directors and manages the center's $5 million budget. He plans to build a $60 million King theme park, which, according to *Ebony* magazine, will use interactive technology, CD-ROMs, holograms, and virtual reality to take visitors back to historic events in the nonviolent movement for civil rights.

It was not easy for Coretta to pass the King legacy on to her son. "I wanted to, but it was hard to let go," Coretta told *Ebony*. "The children refer to the Center as my fifth child. But once I made the decision, I felt relief and inner peace."

Coretta still reports to the office to handle her business affairs. Her personal staff arranges speaking engagements and coordinates travel plans. Coretta's health is good, and she continues to lead a busy— although more private—life.

Simply being Coretta Scott King, however, guarantees that she will always be in the public eye to some degree. She has been a careful guardian of her late husband's speeches and writings; the King estate's reluctance to allow outsiders to use his words or likeness has provoked criticism in the past. Scholars and filmmakers have had to pay the King family for permission to quote or portray Martin in their works. Dexter King has stated that such tight control is necessary to preserve the dignity of his father by discouraging the spread of "the top-40 version" of him, in which the slain leader is exploited on the basis of a few quotable lines from his sermons.

But Coretta and her children may at last be ready to share the vast treasury of Martin's words with the world—on their terms. In 1997, Time Warner, Inc. announced "a multimillion dollar deal" with the King family that would include tape recordings of his speeches, a volume of his sermons—some never before transcribed—and new editions of five books written by King.

As part of the deal, Coretta is also slated to write a new autobiography.

One ongoing drama in the nearly 30 years since the publication of Coretta's first autobiography is the mystery surrounding James Earl Ray, the man

"I wanted to, but it was hard to let go," Coretta told an interviewer of her decision to phase herself out of leadership of the King Center. Here she hugs her son Dexter Scott after naming him the center's new president on April 4, 1989: she would retain the title of CEO until late 1994, however.

convicted of assassinating Martin Luther King Jr. In 1969, Ray pleaded guilty to King's murder before the case ever got to court; after receiving a 99-year sentence, he recanted his confession. Sixty-nine years old and suffering from serious liver disease in 1997, Ray succeeded in getting the King family's support in his repeated petitions for a trial. During a 1997 broadcast of the ABC Television investigative program *Turning Point*, Coretta and her children stated their belief that Ray did not act alone in Martin's murder, but was part of a larger plot.

As spokesman for the Martin Luther King Jr. Center for Nonviolent Social Change, Dexter King has explained his family's reasons for supporting Ray's efforts: "I don't think a trial—if he's granted a trial—will give us the unequivocal truth. But at least we'll know more than we do now."

Coretta has lived with the uncertainty surrounding her husband's death for nearly three decades. While keeping her family strong in the face of tragedy, she has also continued to nurture Martin's dream of racial and economic equality for all Americans. Perhaps the events of April 30, 1993, best demonstrate the depth of Coretta's personal commitment to keeping this dream alive. On that date, the King children, their family, friends, and supporters paid tribute to Coretta for her life's contributions to civil and human rights. A film about the civil-rights struggle was shown. The audience watched in silence as Dr. Martin Luther King Jr. spoke about his wife. "I wish I could say, and satisfy my masculine ego, that I led her down this path," King said. "But we walked down this path together."

Coretta's eyes filled with tears.

CHRONOLOGY

1927	Born Coretta Scott in Heiberger, Alabama
1945	Graduates as valedictorian from segregated Lincoln High School; enters Antioch College on scholarship
1951	Graduates from Antioch; enters New England Conservatory of Music
1952	Meets Martin Luther King Jr.
1953	Marries Martin Luther King Jr. in Marion, Alabama
1954	Graduates from New England Conservatory of Music; moves to Montgomery, Alabama, with Martin
1955	Gives birth to Yolanda Denise King; Montgomery bus boycott begins
1956	The King home is firebombed; racial segregation on Montgomery buses is declared illegal; Coretta stages a concert to raise funds for the Montgomery Improvement Association (MIA)
1957	Standing in for Martin, Coretta attends a meeting of black ministers in Atlanta; the Southern Christian Leadership Conference (SCLC) is formed at a follow-up meeting in New Orleans; son Martin Luther King III is born
1958	Makes first solo public speaking appearance on Women's Day at New Hope Baptist Church in Denver, Colorado; Martin is stabbed in Harlem
1959	Travels to India with Martin
1960	Moves to Atlanta with Martin; joins Women's International League for Peace and Freedom
1961	Gives birth to Dexter Scott King
1962	Travels to Geneva, Switzerland, as part of an international delegation of 50 women to lobby for a ban on atomic weapons testing
1963	Gives birth to Bernice Albertine King; participates in the March on Washington for Jobs and Freedom; President John F. Kennedy is assassinated

1964	Performs the first in a series of Freedom Concerts to raise funds for the SCLC's civil-rights causes; accompanies Martin to Oslo, Norway, where he receives the Nobel Peace Prize
1965	Enrolls her two oldest children in a previously all-white public school in Atlanta
1966	Moves with family to a public housing unit in Chicago as part of a campaign against urban poverty; helps found Women Mobilized for Change to help city residents improve their living conditions
1968	Martin Luther King Jr. assassinated in Memphis, Tennessee; Coretta appears in his place on Solidarity Day at the Lincoln Memorial, making a historic speech of her own; announces plans to build Martin Luther King Center for Nonviolent Social Change
1969	Travels to Italy and India; receives Italian government's Universal Love Award and visits the Vatican; accepts India's Nehru Award on behalf of Martin; visits England and becomes first woman to give sermon at St. Paul's Cathedral in London; leads striking hospital workers on march in Charleston, South Carolina; Coretta's autobiography, *My Life with Martin Luther King Jr.*, is published; American Library Association establishes Coretta Scott King Book Award for children's literature
1982	Opens Martin Luther King Center for Nonviolent Social Change to the public
1983	Attends signing ceremony as President Ronald Reagan makes Martin Luther King's birthday a national holiday
1986	Leads King holiday march in Atlanta to mark first official observance
1990	Welcomes Nelson Mandela to America during a rally in Atlanta following his release from prison
1994	Steps down as CEO and president of King Center; appoints son Dexter to replace her
1997	King estate and Time Warner, Inc. make deal to publish King's speeches and writings, plus new autobiography by Coretta; Coretta and children publicly support motion for retrial of convicted King assassin James Earl Ray

FURTHER READING

Garrow, David J. "Pointing Toward a Plot." Newsweek, February 17, 1997, 55.

_____ . *Bearing the Cross: Martin Luther King, Jr. and the Southern Christian Leadership Conference*. New York: William Morrow, 1986.

Giddings, Paula. *When and Where I Enter: The Impact of Black Women on Race and Sex in America*. New York: William Morrow, 1984.

Harris, Art. "Carrying on the Dream." *Washington Post*, January 19, 1986.

Jones, Malcolm Jr. "A Multimedia 'Dream.'" *Newsweek*, January 20, 1997, 66.

King, Coretta Scott. *My Life with Martin Luther King, Jr*. Rev. ed.
New York: Henry Holt and Company, 1993.

Patterson, Lillie. *Coretta Scott King*. Easton, MD: Garrard Publishing Company, 1977.

Vivian, Octavia. *Coretta: The Story of Mrs. Martin Luther King, Jr*. Philadelphia: Fortress Press, 1970.

White, Jack E. "The Mysteries of James Earl Ray." *Time*, February 17, 1997, 73.

Williams, Juan. "Coretta's Way." *Washington Post*, June 4, 1989.

The Words of Martin Luther King Jr. Selected by Coretta Scott King. New York: Newmarket Press, 1983.

INDEX

PICTURE CREDITS

LISA RENEE RHODES is a graduate of Bernard M. Baruch College, City University of New York, and the Columbia Graduate School of Journalism. She is a writer and reviewer of literature for children and young adults.

NATHAN IRVIN HUGGINS, one of America's leading scholars in the field of black studies, helped select the titles for the BLACK AMERICANS OF ACHIEVEMENT series, for which he also served as senior consulting editor. He was the W. E. B. Du Bois Professor of History and Afro-American Studies at Harvard University and the director of the W. E. B. Du Bois Institute for Afro-American Research at Harvard. He received his doctorate from Harvard in 1962 and returned there as professor in 1980 after teaching at Columbia University, the University of Massachusetts, Lake Forest College, and the California State University, Long Beach. He was the author of four books and dozens of articles, including *Black Odyssey: The Afro-American Ordeal in Slavery*, *The Harlem Renaissance*, and *Slave and Citizen: The Life of Frederick Douglass*, and was associated with the Children's Television Workshop, National Public Radio, the Boston Athenaeum, the Museum of Afro-American History, the Howard Thurman Educational Trust, and Upward Bound. Professor Huggins died in 1989, at the age of 62, in Cambridge, Massachusetts.